DATE DUE 8

OCT 2 3 2014			

Demco

Information Technology, Development, and Social Change

Routledge Studies in Development and Society

Information Technology, Development, and Social Change

Edited by Fay Patel, Prahalad Sooknanan, Giselle Rampersad, and Anuradha Mundkur

Routledge
Taylor & Francis Group
NEW YORK   LONDON

First published 2012
by Routledge
711 Third Avenue, New York, NY 10017

Simultaneously published in the UK
by Routledge
2 Park Square, Milton Park, Abingdon, Oxon OX14 4RN

Routledge is an imprint of the Taylor & Francis Group,
an informa business

© 2012 Taylor & Francis

The right of Fay Patel, Prahalad Sooknanan, Giselle Rampersad, and
Anuradha Mundkur to be identified as the authors of the editorial material,
and of the authors for their individual chapters, has been asserted in
accordance with sections 77 and 78 of the Copyright, Designs and Patents
Act 1988.

Library of Congress Cataloging-in-Publication Data
   Information technology, development, and social change / edited by Fay
Patel . . . [et al.].
      p. cm. — (Routledge studies in development and society ; 32)
   Includes bibliographical references and index.
   1. Information technology.   2. Economic development.   3. Digital
divide.   4. Social change.   I. Patel, Fay.
   HC79.I55I53935 2012
   303.48'33—dc23
   2011042898

ISBN13: 978-0-415-50268-9 (hbk)
ISBN13: 978-0-203-12120-7 (ebk)

Typeset in Sabon
by IBT Global.

Printed and bound in the United States of America on sustainably sourced
paper by IBT Global.

We dedicate this book to developing communities around the world who struggle against the odds and who aspire to a higher quality of life for themselves and their children. Our book is also dedicated to our parents and to their parents upon whom various injustices were inflicted in the name of development through centuries of colonization, and imperialism, and what may be termed bonded development.

****

I dedicate this book to my husband Feisal and our son Farhaan, to my late parents, Ahmed and Amina Essack Gangat; my brothers Golam Gangat and Yusuf Gangat; and my sisters Bilkis Mohamed Kara, Fawzia Haroon Master, and Khairoonisa Yusuf Hatia who live in Durban, South Africa. I am grateful to them for the lessons they taught me about never faltering in adversity and embracing destiny with a strong spirit of resilience. My deep faith in God has always guided me in striving for fairness and justice in all things.

Fay (Feiziya) Patel

I dedicate this book to my wife Val, daughter Shiveta, and son Shival whom I thank for their ongoing support, love, and patience during the years that I studied in the United Kingdom and the United States. The book is also dedicated to my late father, Babwah Sooknanan and late mother, Kowsil Sooknanan.

Prahalad Sooknanan

I dedicate this book to my dear love, Brendan Duffy, our son James Francis, my parents Richard and Gail, and my sister Ria Rampersad who have been a tremendous source of inspiration, support, and love. Above all, I give thanks to God who leads me through my mission.

Giselle Rampersad

Dedicated to my grandfather: You have been an inspiration to all your grandchildren; your love and support have seen me through some of my toughest challenges. Also dedicated to my father who did not live to see this dream come true and my mother and family for their undying faith in me and my husband Ravi for being the wind beneath my wings.

Anuradha Mundkur

Contents

PART I

Alternative Perspectives on the Diffusion of Innovations and International Development

PART II

Innovative Technology: Impact on Developing Communities

PART III

International Development: Critical Perspectives on Health,
Poverty and Environment

Figures and Tables

FIGURES

TABLES

Foreword
Beyond the Innovation Divide

Southern countries and communities are increasingly affected by the modernization recipe of economic growth by either donor countries or donor agencies (such as the World Bank or the International Monetary Fund), which implies the retreat of the state in favor of various forms of privatization. These policies operate within the umbrella of international development as foreign aid hand-outs to developing communities. After an extensive assessment of international aid policies and projects, the former World Bank economist William Easterly (2006) reaches the conclusion that "sixty years of countless reform schemes to aid agencies and dozens of different plans, and $2.3 trillion later, the aid industry is still failing to reach the beautiful goal [of making poverty history]. The evidence points to an unpopular conclusion: Big Plans will always fail to reach the beautiful goal" (p. 11).

However, from a Southern governmental perspective there appears to be a general concern to miss the so-called information revolution, and as a consequence the majority of policy decisions relate to the spending of public funds on the acquisition of the latest generation of computers and new technology in general. In other words, most of the Southern governments fear to remain 'backward' and therefore often overlook the specific socio-economic and socio-cultural contexts in which technology transfer has to be considered. Many Western and Southern policymakers alike seem to assume that technical and economic progress is simply a means to an end and that it hardly affects the culture in which it occurs. It seems to me as if they believe that they can achieve Western-style progress and at the same time retain their culture and their morals or, at the least, most of the essential parts of them. In other words, they don't question the assumptions on which the diffusion of innovations model is based.

At a theoretical level, this perspective is referred to as the *modernization paradigm* and *diffusion of innovations model* (Servaes, 1999, 2008). Both maintain that technology produced in the West is appropriate to the needs of developing countries and that the most efficient and adequate mechanism for transferring this technology is commercially, through transnational corporations. The rationale for this strategy is based on the proposition that (a) commercial technology transfer through transnational corporations offer all necessary combinations of technology components within a complete system of technology development and transfer, and (b) technology transfer needed to establish any new productive facility is a complicated process, requiring special knowledge and skills for each stage of its development. Moreover, this viewpoint claims that the alleged success of transnational firms in transferring technology is due not only to their mastery of the whole 'technology package' but also to the fact that this package is closely integrated with management, marketing, and financing skills. As a consequence one argues that any attempt to separate elements of technology transfer will either fail or result in considerably larger 'costs'.

To technology is attributed a direct impact on the economic development, the political organization, and socio-cultural value system of a society. However, what these perspectives don't seem to acknowledge is that technology is called into existence by a particular set of historical circumstances that shape and define that technology. One must understand that set of historical circumstances if one is to comprehend the effective *relationship between technology and society.* Contrary to popular belief, technology is not politically neutral or value free; technology definitely determines the socio-cultural structure and communication patterns of a given society. In other words, Western technology cannot be adopted without taking in aspects of Western culture at the same time. In my opinion, science and technology are much more than the mere instruments they were expected to be; they cannot be borrowed or bought.

Therefore there are at least three *implicit basic values* in Western technology (Hofstede & Hofstede, 2005). First, Western technology shows little respect for myth, symbol, or the power of the mysterious. Every phenomenon has to be broken down into component parts, tested and verified. Second, the technology is based on the cult of efficiency. The central considerations are productivity, cost-benefit ratio, and the bottom line. Third, the technology dominates and manipulates nature rather than being in harmony with it. Problem solving is the goal; hence, reality is reduced to those dimensions which can be studied as problems needing solutions. The values implicit in Western technology may therefore come into conflict with the pre-existing values of a non-Western environment.

Furthermore, science and technology penetrate other subsystems of society as well. They are a whole system of explanation, which affects not only science and technology but also seemingly unconnected areas like positive law and a modern government and bureaucracy where traditional ascriptions, hierarchies, and authorities are replaced by so-called objective standards and decision making.

What is refreshing about this book is that the authors view international development through the lens of socio-economic and political realities of Southern countries and communities in general, and of those in India, Trinidad & Tobago, and South Africa in particular. According to the authors, 'questions of access, privilege, illiteracy, injustice, and poverty, among others, remain key concerns as developing communities struggle with issues of train-ing, utilization, implementation, and the unexpected consequences of adopt-ing new technology' (p. xix).

The authors argue that *social responsibility, accountability, justice, and sustainability* were absent from earlier models, and this absence continues to be noted in the 21st century when the demographics of the global population has shifted and the needs and demands of global communities beg a more sensitive, appropriate response to improve the quality of life and well-being of developing communities that are operating within and across various geo-graphical boundaries, because, as Nobel Prize winner Amartya Sen (2004) argues, 'The deciding issue, ultimately, has to be one of democracy. An over-arching value must be the need for participatory decision-making on the kind of society people want to live in, based on open discussion, with adequate opportunity for the expression of minority positions' (p. 20).

The authors challenge the notion that innovations in communication media, particularly the effective use of new information and communication technologies, mean progress and advancement for the developing communi-ties and that the gaps of access and rights have been bridged. To the contrary, whereas developing communities try to grapple with the digital divide, a new divide is approaching: the innovation divide. Scenarios presented analyze the ways in which the diffusion of new communication technologies either aids or obstructs their progress and advancement on the international develop-ment front.

I fully endorse the editors' argument that a new world order should be based on a more multilateral and collective perspective of 'a *sustainable soci-ety* that embraces justice, equality, respect, and dignity' (p. xviii).

According to Juan Pérez de Cuéllar (1995), chairing the UNESCO World Commission on Culture and Development, the basic principle should be one of *cultural respect*: the fostering of respect for all cultures whose values are tolerant of others. Respect goes beyond tolerance and implies a positive atti-tude to other people and a rejoicing in their culture. Social peace is neces-sary for human development: in turn it requires that differences between cultures be regarded not as something alien and unacceptable or hateful, but as experiments in ways of living together that contain valuable lessons and information for all. (p. 25)

As noted by the authors (p. 13), 'redressing the injustices of modernity requires the revitalization of a social consciousness that invokes socially just frameworks to uplift the quality of life for developing communities within and across developed and developing world contexts '.

Jan Servaes
UNESCO Chair in Communication for Sustainable Social Change
Director of the Centre for Communication and Social Change,
College of Social and Behavioral Sciences,University of Massachusetts,
Amherst

REFERENCES

Easterly, W. (2006). *The white man's burden. Why the West's efforts to aid the rest have done so much ill and so little good.* New York: Penguin Books.

Hofstede, G. H., & Hofstede, G. J. (2005). *Cultures and organizations. Software of the mind.* London: McGraw-Hill.

Pérez de Cuéllar, J. P. (1995). *Our creative diversity: Report of the World Commission on Culture and Development.* Paris: UNESCO.

Sen, A. (2000). *Development as freedom.* New York: Anchor Books.

Sen, A. (2004). Cultural liberty and human development. In S. Fukuda-Parr (Ed.), *Human development report: Cultural liberty in today's diverse world.* New York: United Nations Development Programme.

Servaes, J. (1999). *Communication for development. One world, multiple cultures.* Cresskill, NJ: Hampton Press.

Servaes, J. (Ed.). (2008). *Communication for development and social change.* Thousand Oaks, CA: Sage.

Preface

Our perception with respect to diffusion of innovation is influenced by the research and work of Western scholars (e.g., Lerner, 1958; Rogers, 1995; Schramm, 1964) from the old tradition who pioneered diffusion of innovations theory in the early to mid-20th century. Our understanding of international development is shaped by the traditional frameworks of importing and exporting diffusion of innovations between developed and developing communities in the early to mid-20th century; by our own experiences as international students and as immigrants in a developed community context; and simultaneously, by our legitimate status as members of developing communities. We view international development through the lens of our socio-economic and political realities (past and present) in South Africa, Trinidad & Tobago, and India over the latter part of the last century.

The merits of the theoretical frameworks on diffusion of innovations and international development that are emerging in the developed community (formerly the West, the First World, the North, developed nation) and the equally important grassroots perspectives of the developing community (formerly the South, the Third World, developing nations and world, and underdeveloped/ less developed world) are acknowledged as fundamental to our understanding of the imbalance of power between the communities. Various terms and labels are used to describe the dichotomized worldview. However, the editors prefer the terms *developing* and *developed* communities as a substitute for the former labels mentioned earlier. In our view, this terminology encourages readers to transcend geographical barriers and to move within the realm of the virtual spaces created by information and communication technologies (ICTs) and other spaces that have been contested by many migrant communities as they cross territorial borders and enter new lands for study and work in order to embrace a better quality of life. With the rapid increase in migration around the world these past few decades, developing communities are everywhere.

Developing communities comprise citizens of the world who also live in the backyards of developed communities and who continue to be marginalized and impoverished in spite of industrialization and globalization. They remain in the shadowed ghettoes of the developed world. Developing communities face unrelenting indignities and deep disrespect to their person, their families, their indigenous knowledge, and their histories. We envisage a new era in which they will experience an alternative form of innovation diffusion and international development that will uplift their spirit, celebrate their ancestry, and embrace their humanity so that future generations can benefit from their collective strength.

Against this conundrum, we subscribe to the view that another dimension must be posited in attaining a new world order that is no longer dichotomized by economic power and status but that is more multilateral in its collective vision of a sustainable society that embraces justice, respect, and dignity. Consequently, we write from our perspectives as critical scholars of mass communication who struggle on a regular basis with the tensions of crossing the divide between the developing and the developed community contexts in which our reality is embedded. We have to critically assess our standpoints as we move precariously within and outside the two communities, always remaining on the periphery. This book, therefore, attests to our ongoing dilemmas as products of a developed community belonging to the old world order as we continue to struggle for acceptance as legitimate contributors to the developing community heritages which we embrace in everything we do.

In this book, we create a space for researchers to explore these concepts from their peculiar vantage points, particularly noting that authors bring their own unique worldviews. Of special focus in this book is the courage of four colleagues to co-edit a book that contests old worldviews on technology and development. More importantly, all of the editors defy the norm when it comes to speaking from 'inside another skin' and maintaining that their individual and collective voices are significant in a new century. Further, we have invited authors from   a range of cultural contexts to share their critical perspectives on the diffusion of new ICTs and on international development with the aim of presenting inclusive yet diverse points of view.

Chapters in the book cover a wide range of issues related to the diffusion of ICTs and international development and highlight critical issues that are unique to developing and developed communities alike. The speed and cost-effectiveness of new information technologies have prompted many to view these innovations as a panacea for social and economic development. However, such a view flies in the face of continuing inequities in education, health, food, and infrastructure. As a result, we must challenge deterministic notions that innovations in communication media, particularly the effective use of new ICTs, mean progress and advancement for the developing communities and that the gaps of access and rights have (and can be) been bridged.

The adoption of new ICTs, such as the Internet, computer software and hardware, HDTV, cellular and satellite communication, by developing communities create a false reality that these communities are more advanced and better educated in the 21st century than ever before. In fact, critical studies looking historically at the diffusion of innovations and the real-life experiences indicate that an escalation in the adoption of new communication technologies does not necessarily mean that global communities are better informed and more advanced. Questions of access, privilege, illiteracy, and poverty, among others, remain key concerns as developing communities struggle with issues of training, utilization, implementation, and the unexpected consequences of adopting new technology. For instance, consequences of the adoption of new communication technologies in relation to the environment and health of the developing communities are often ignored and remain a contentious issue between developed and developing nations.

The challenges posed by meaningful diffusion, therefore, provoke obvious questions. Do developing communities have the necessary training and education with regard to new technologies? Do they have access to the new technologies? What are some of the assumptions that are made about the diffusion of new technologies, and why and how do these affect the exchange of information among developing communities? In what ways does the diffusion of new communication technologies contribute further to the social injustices of poverty, disease, illiteracy, and inequality of power and wealth?

The primary goal of this book is to encourage readers to critically examine the aforementioned questions with a view to creating a more equitable space for developing communities who strive against all odds on a daily basis to improve their quality of life. Scenarios presented in the chapters from developing community perspectives testify to the ways in which the diffusion of new communication technologies either aids or obstructs their progress and advancement on the international development front. They will highlight the hidden agendas that drive the diffusion of technology and the costs associated with not recognizing the pitfalls of technologization.

The book is divided into three parts. Part I introduces alternative paradigms on the diffusion of innovations and international development; Part II explores the impact of innovative technology on developing communities; and Part III highlights critical perspectives of international development on health, poverty, and the environment.

The contributing authors of this book have shared valuable insights and offered reasonable proposals and suggestions that could support a range of organizations in the public and private sectors as well as in academia. Policymakers from both the developed and the developing community contexts would find these proposals of interest. In particular, international development officials, innovation and technology decision makers, and those responsible for strategic research and development investment would benefit from these insights given the balanced perspective provided by authors of both developed and developing contexts. Further, managers of multinational companies that span both developed and developing regions can better understand the innovation diffusion impact on the quality of life of these communities.

Co-editing a book among four co-editors in two countries and working with contributing authors in other countries is a complex task. Coordinating the authorships for the book proved a challenge especially when each contributor experienced multiple issues that affected the status of their work life, family, and health. Nevertheless, their spirit and commitment remained firm in the hope that this book will be a significant contribution to the already vast literature on innovative diffusion and international development, particularly in providing an alternative viewpoint. It is the fortitude of the co-editors and authors to give currency to the 'other' voice and their collective stand against traditional exploitive paradigms that brings to this book a subversive flavor. The underlying goals of this book are to explore alternative paradigms and critical perspectives of innovation diffusion and international development more vociferously. Our stance is unconventional and it is our conviction that it is time to examine these dimensions with candor. Our hope is to see a diverse range of alternative paradigms emerge and to hear a crescendo of critical voices rise around the globe and reach critical mass so that social justice, human and sustainable development will never again be absent in innovation diffusion and international development discourse.

Emerging alternative models of diffusion of innovations and international development must commit to human development, social responsibility and justice and sustainable outcomes for developing and developed communities. Our search for alternative models must revive a liberation discourse of international development that will inevitably free developing communities from their colonial shackles. We have an obligation to create a space in which our children will again be embraced with dignity and respect and who will in turn embrace humanity with a renewed spirit of love and humility.

Fay Patel
Prahalad Sooknanan
Giselle Rampersad
Anuradha Mundkur

REFERENCES

Lerner, D. (1958). *The passing of traditional society: Modernizing the Middle East.* New York: Free Press.
Rogers, E. M. (1995). *Diffusion of innovations* (5th ed.). New York: Free Press.
Schramm, W. (1964). *Mass media and national development.* Stanford, CA: Stanford University Press.

Acknowledgments

We are deeply indebted to our contributing authors without whom this book would not have become a reality. Their interest and commitment to the book project spurred us on in achieving our dream. We thank them for sharing our visions for a human-oriented paradigm of information technology, development, and social change.

We are also honored to have Professor Jan Servaes write the *Foreword* to the book. Jan is the UNESCO Chair in Communication for Sustainable Social Change. He is also the Director of the Centre for Communication and Social Change within the College of Social and Behavioral Sciences at the University of Massachusetts, Amherst. His international reputation as an outstanding scholar of communication and international development has inspired us over the decades.

We thank our colleagues, friends, and acquaintances who provided support and many hours of enlightening conversations over the years about the unjust development practices across a wide range of communities around the world. These conversations, along with our own experiences helped us to understand that innovation diffusion and international development in a developing community context can be a destructive force to be contested in every space on an ongoing basis, unless it is designed to be culturally appropriate and respectful and implemented in accordance with the principles of equity and integrity.

We are grateful to Max Novick, Jennifer Morrow at Routledge USA and to Michael Watters and his editorial team for their guidance and advice in successfully concluding the project.

****

Fay is indebted to her three co-editors: Prahalad Sooknanan, with whom the idea for the book was first brainstormed nearly 5 years ago; Giselle Rampersad and Anuradha Mundkur, who were bold enough to join this venture in the last two years before publication and who revitalized the dream once more to bring it to fruition. The collective ongoing encouragement and support of the co-editors, despite their own personal and health challenges, made it possible for the book to develop into reality in a short space of time. Fay acknowledges the assistance of Kay Govin (University of Adelaide, South Australia) and is deeply appreciative of her willingness to review the manuscript in the final stages of preparation for publication. Fay is grateful to her husband Feisal and her son Farhaan for their hours of patience and support as personal consultants and advisors on technology related matters.

* * * * * * * * * * *

Prahalad wishes to acknowledge the assistance of the Organization of the American States for the award of a doctoral fellowship to read for the degree in Mass Communication at Bowling Green State University. He is grateful to SUNY, College at Potsdam for the opportunity to teach courses in communication, thus reinforcing his interest in the field. Prahalad expresses his gratitude to the Arthur Lok Jack Graduate School of Business, University of the West Indies, University of Trinidad and Tobago, and the University of Leicester where he teaches a variety of communication courses. He is indebted to them for sustaining his interest in the field by supervising graduate students and engaging in research publications. Prahalad is also grateful to the lead author, Fay Patel for the opportunity to co-edit this book.

* * * * * * * * * * *

Giselle commends the hard work and dedication of the editors Fay, Prahalad, and Anuradha. She also thanks Fay Patel for the opportunity to co-edit the book and to all of the contributing authors for their valuable insights and commitment. Giselle also acknowledges Flinders University for creating opportunities for her to coordinate degrees and courses in technology and innovation and in supporting her research in innovation. Giselle thanks the University of Adelaide for sponsoring her PhD and to Durham University for kindling her passion for innovation. She acknowledges her vibrant students that continue to inspire her to learn.

* * * * * * * * * * *

Anuradha would like to thank her mentors, Associate Professor Murali Venkatesh (Adviser and Chair of her PhD committee), Professor Milton Mueller, Assistant Professor Jon Gant and Assistant Professor Diana Burley, for their support and encouragement; her friends for giving their moral support; and her co-editors Fay, Prahalad, and Giselle for the opportunity to co-edit the book with them.

* * * * * * * * * * *

Part I

Alternative Perspectives on the Diffusion of Innovations and International Development

Traditional paradigms of the diffusion of innovations and international development were designed and implemented to modernize and civilize the developing communities as a desired goal. Of course, another less articulated goal was to increase the economic prosperity of Western nations which was done under the guise of knowledge transfer initiatives – between the developed and the developing communities. These models were exported during the mid to end of the last century as industrialization and modernization packages from the Western nations. In the developing community context, recipients of the innovation and development initiatives spoke out about the incompatibility of these development initiatives with their indigenous knowledge, cultural values and beliefs, and various aspects of sustainable development. However, the voices of developing communities remained insignificant whispers in the wind because Western superpowers like the United States of America, Britain and some European countries had a remarkable hegemonic influence on the global political economy. Alternative paradigms advocating for a human-centred perspective in development that respect and value the cultural and indigenous knowledge of developing communities were ignored and dismissed.

The authors of the introductory chapters reiterate the call for human-centred alternative paradigms that respect and value cultural and indigenous knowledge and suggest that it is imperative that innovation diffusion and international development in the 21st century take cognizance of the need to design and implement innovative development that will consider human and sustainable development as the ultimate goal. In chapter one, Patel, Rampersad and Sooknanan retrace the history of innovation diffusion and international development and make a bold attempt to seek some form of justice for the wrongs that modernity has imposed on developing communities. They contend that many atrocities have been inflicted upon developing communities in the past in the name of modernization and industrialization and that the current trends in technologization and globalization have the same agendas. Next, Patel implores practitioners, sponsors, and agencies to re-establish socially responsible, just, and sustainable goals and agendas so that the human development component is fully supported and resourced in all future initiatives. Rampersad further develops the theme of empowerment and calls for a holistic approach to the diffusion of innovations. Particularly, the chapter provides a framework for sustainable innovation that will allow developing communities to drive the innovation in tandem with their goals for a sustained future.

1 Diffusing the Innovation Divide in International Development
Redressing the Injustices of Modernity

Fay Patel, Giselle Rampersad, and Prahalad Sooknanan

INTRODUCTION

In the early part of the 20th century, there was a notable trend in modernizing the world through industrial development. Both the superpowers and the developing communities were striving to win the race or to catch up with industrialization in an effort to be seen as industrialized nations that were committed to a modern, higher quality of life for their citizens. In the 21st century, that same fervor to modernize has emerged once more with a renewed vigor, but this time there is an urgency to technologize. In other words, the goals and dreams to keep the world chugging along on the old steam engine have suddenly moved forward at lightning speed to digitize an already modern and industrial economy bringing information and communication fast forward into the 21st century.

This chapter will critically assess if technologization and globalization have replaced the old paradigm of modernization and industrialization and, if so, in what ways. The authors identify the old socio-economic and political tensions and divisions in the current traditional paradigm and offer alternative perspectives which bring unique challenges. They subscribe to the view that the new century calls for a more candid statement on the elimination of the socio-economic and political divide within and across the developed and developing community contexts in an attempt to redress the injustices that were delivered in the name of modernity.

HISTORICAL OVERVIEW

Communication technologies have long been lauded for their potential as development tools (Lerner, 1958; Schramm, 1964). In the same vein, Rogers (1969) maintained that the mass media have the capacity to bridge the gap between tradition and modernity and are 'magic multipliers' in the process of social change. Indeed, these were the Western notions of development that constituted the dominant paradigm of development during the 1950s and 1960s. By the 1970s, however, the dominant paradigm of development had fallen short of expectations (Rogers, 1976). In other words, the Western theories that supported the direct and powerful effects of the mass media had failed to yield meaningful results in the developing countries context. In fact, instead of being a significant variable in the development process, the mass media were blamed for increasing the knowledge gap between the advantaged and disadvantaged communities in the developing nations (referred to as the 'Third World' in the literature in previous decades). Mody (1991) attributed this failure to the unwitting disregard for the Third World (developing community) context with regard to their social, psychological, political, and economic environment.

In the aftermath of the dominant paradigm, emerging technologies ushered in a new era in development and the role of information and communication technologies (ICTs) in particular. ICTs, otherwise known as 'new media', held promise for corresponding changes in the nature of human communication and social change. These assumptions were premised on the fact that new communication technologies are interactive (can 'talk back' to the user), de-massified (can individualize the exchange of information), asynchronous (can send and receive messages at convenient times to the user), and also synchronous as more people expect immediate and real-time response via the ICTs as they do over the telephone and in person. In other words, new media were perceived as having the unique ability to transcend temporal and spatial constraints as well as facilitate collaboration and participatory communication (Rogers, 1986). The advent of new communication technologies or ICTs, therefore, heralded a new wave of optimism in national development. In contrast with traditional mass media communication, Stover (1984) upheld that ICTs go further by offering possibilities for change and new perspectives for development. More specifically, ICTs were seen as having tremendous potential for improving development initiatives in areas such as health, science, agriculture, and education associating it with uplifting the economic wellbeing of people and leading to the eradication of poverty among developing communities.

Notwithstanding the touted benefits, tangible results from development potentials did not materialize for a variety of reasons. For one thing, the concept of development remained ambiguous in social and economic thought. Fagerlind and Saha (1989) claimed that development was used interchangeably with social change, growth, advancement, and modernization. More critically, they claimed that, with the exception of the term *social change*, the others imply change in a specific direction, which is regarded by users as positive or highly valued. In retrospect, this was consistent with the positive and uni-linear bias of development which strongly influenced the European or Western model of development that was deployed to restore war-torn Europe. Development later became known as Westernization or Europeanization (Mowlana & Wilson, 1988).

Given the success of the Western model of development during the 1950s and early 1960s, Western scholars were led to believe that this feat could be duplicated among the newly independent nations that emerged among the developing communities. Indeed, their optimism was misguided because this model of development was influenced by events such as the Industrial Revolution, the colonial experience of the Third World, dominant quantitative empiricism, and prevailing economic and political thinking (Rogers, 1976). Melkote (1991), concurs with this view outlining that this dominant paradigm of development advocated economic growth through industrialization, introduction of capital-intensive technology, capital formation by saving money and sacrifice of short-term goals for long-term ones, a top-down structure of authority, and a 'modern' mindset among individuals. By the late 1960s and 1970s, it was not surprising that the Western models of development had failed among Third World (developing community) countries (Mowlana & Wilson, 1988). Melkote (1991) criticized this alien model of development for its pro-economic bias and quantifiable variables, neglecting labor-intensive strategies, ignoring constraints imposed from outside, supporting a top-down approach to planning and development, overlooking the socio-cultural context showing lack of concern for self-reliance and participation in development activities. In retrospect, Eisenstadt (1976) lamented that the dominant paradigm of development succeeded more as a description of social change in Western Europe and North America than as a predictor of change in developing countries.

Evidently, the failure of Western models of development can be attributed to their inappropriateness and false assumptions. To this end, Fagerlind and Saha (1989) argue that difficulties arise when one attempts to extrapolate alien economic growth models to countries with different socio-cultural values and structures and whose resources preclude normal strategies for industrialization. They further contend that these models assume that a number of key variables will remain constant, when in fact they can be unpredictable. In contrast, the success of an economic growth model is dependent upon growth, capital accumulation, motives to maximize profits, and the improvement in general conditions of life. In other words, the ideal economic model turns out to be partly sociological as well as psychological.

Nearly over half a century after the rush to modernize and industrialize the world and, particularly, to export diffusion of innovations to the developing communities around the world, we are standing once more on the edge of another phenomenal revolution: technologization. New sophisticated information and communication technologies are emerging at greater speed than before. The range of technology and growing network access capabilities include

a) Laptops, Notebooks, Netbooks, and Tablets now available for mobile use
b) Internet and email access through Wifi and Fibre Optic networks

  c) Smartphones that provide multiple communication services such as email, text messaging, banking and document exchange
  d) HDTV with its revolutionary picture clarity and 3DTV with Wi-Fi and Internet capabilities
  e) Social media options such as Facebook and Twitter and their integration and constant presence in all aspects of life.

The rapid increase in the variety of digital media options and rate of diffusion is having an overwhelming effect on ordinary people. At the same time, technologization is continuing to divide the world into those who can afford these technologies and digital gadgets ('the haves' or 'the rich') and those who cannot ('the have nots' or 'the poor'). The notion of modernization in the last century also further divided the developing communities into the 'haves' and the 'have not'.

McMichael (2004, p. 22) is of the view that President Truman's proclamation in the late 1940s further 'divided the world between those who were modern and those who were not'. Modernization was associated with notions of becoming more like the Western superpowers (such as the United States and Britain) through an increase in ownership of and access to machinery. Today, technologization is viewed in a similar light and so communities around the world continue to trample over each other to adopt a new technology as it arrives on the market. For example, adopting the Apple manufactured iPhone and then the iPad within months of its appearance is only one example of how fast the new technologies are diffusing and being consumed by developed and developing communities alike. More recently, the scramble for an iPhone 4S (Clark, 2011) was a global event in October 2011 when people worldwide were lining up in the streets from California and Paris to Sydney and Tokyo with some people camping out in front of stores for up to two and three nights to be first at the iPhone 4S launch. This event along with other media evidence of the 'technology wars' among the corporations to monopolize the electronics industry demonstrates the speed with which new technology is emerging and diffusing. Corporations like Research in Motion (RIM) and Apple continue to compete at all levels. Ganapati (2009) identifies access to support and application development as two of the many challenges facing RIM as it competes with Apple. Service blackouts in October 2011 caused RIM further setbacks and Apple's launch of ' the latest version of its mobile operating system, iOS 5, available to iPhone users' at that same time caused more harm to RIM's corporate image and to confidence levels among consumers, according to Hartley (2011). Worthham (2011) cites a recent Nielson Survey finding that the adoption of the Smartphone in the USA has increased to 43 percent with 28 percent of Smartphone owners using an iPhone. Android's emerging presence and increased adoption as an alternative platform will further challenge the current dominance of the iPhone on the global market. Competitiveness in the industry will encourage more innovations leading to better technologies. This rapid adoption of new communication technology such as the Smartphone reflects a new wave of technologization in the twenty-first century and brings with it concerns about the further dichotomization of 'those who have and those who do not have ' the means to enter a technologized era.

The assumptions about what was meant by modernization and industrialization in the last century have been transferred to current notions of technologization and globalization. McMichael (2004, p. 23) claims that 'development/modernity became the standard by which other societies were judged'. Communities around the world assume that an increase in ownership and access to machinery and technology equals progress; that a higher level of export and import of machinery and technology means that communities are modernizing and advancing at a faster pace; and that an increase in production and consumption levels among developing communities means that they are reaching the 'desired' socio-economic status with Western nations. Toyama (2010) notes that the ICT4D (Information Communication Technology for Development) research group would have been pleased if technology had a way 'to advance the cause of poverty alleviation' but they found in their 'research projects in multiple domains (education, microfinance, agriculture, health care) and with various technologies (PCs, mobile phones, custom-designed electronics)' that this was not the case. Further, Toyama (2010) claims that "new technologies generate optimism and exuberance eventually dashed by disappointing realities". Issues of unequal interdependence continue, given the imbalance in the flow of income from the adopter to the creator of the technology. McMichael (2004, p. 22), asserts that 'whereas the First World had 65% of the world income with only 20% of the world's population, the Third World accounted for 67% of the world's population but only 18 % of its income'. These figures demonstrate the huge gaps among those who enjoy a higher level of socio-economic status and those who do not. The inequities and tensions arising from the interdependence among developed and developing communities within a global economy context are often not recognized but we must make a concerted effort to respond appropriately to the lived reality of developing communities. In response to the Great Recession and the financial crises of 2008 in the United States, Nayyar (2011, p.20) calls for a rethink of national and global policies "that are conducive to developing countries' because these crises affect the lives of developing communities in complex ways. It is therefore an imperative that technologization does not repeat the errors of the past. Rogers (1995) asserts that 'the fast growth of diffusion studies in the Third World countries in the 1960s occurred because technology was assumed to be the heart of development, at least as development was conceptualized at that time (p.59). It seems from the foregoing discussion that even in a new century technology adoption continues to increase at a rapid rate because of lingering notions of modernity being aligned to technology adoption and use. However, 'development is about the living conditions of ordinary people' (Nayyar, 2011, p.21) and so in a new century we must respond in people-centred and proactive ways to transform the notion of development to one that embraces humanity.

In this chapter, *technologization* is defined as the rapid increase in ownership, access, and dependency on technology. Further, we subscribe to Mosco and Schiller's (2001, p. 89) definition of *globalization* 'as the configuration of the world economy', which they claim 'is understood as the contemporary process of ever greater—and accelerated—articulation and unequal interdependence between countries and world regions' (p. 88). The language of technologization and globalization closely resembles the economic and political patterns and behavior of ownership and dominance that emerged among the superpowers within the old paradigms. It is necessary to examine these patterns to ascertain if we simply have new terms replacing the old. McMichael (2004, p. 292) is of the view that 'global development looks increasingly like a rerun of the colonial era'.

TECHNOLOGIZATION AND GLOBALIZATION: OLD PARADIGM REFRAMED?

According to McMichael (2004, xxiii), 'one of the distinguishing features of the new century is the powerful apparatus of communication that presents an image of a world unified by global technologies and products and their universal appeal.' However, the reality is different in terms of various cultural, economic, and political contexts. In some cases, global communities are living the global dream of accessing and enjoying technological advantages, and in other cases the simple act of owning technology remains a dream. Furthermore, the upsurge of technological advancement and its successful diffusion in some countries create the impression that new ICTs are magical instruments of communication. Based on the literature (for example, Gurumurthy, 2004) and anecdotal evidence, several assumptions are made about the impact and influence of ICTs: ICTs will connect more people more of the time at a faster pace than the older communication technologies did; information will not only be disseminated at a faster pace but that people will become better informed because of the massive database of the new information and communication technologies; ICTs will bridge the divide between the rich and the poor; men and women will communicate on level playing fields in virtual space; and that technologies themselves will diffuse at a rapid pace without much human effort. These assumptions have been researched and refuted (Gurumurthy,2004; Toyama, 2010 and Nayyar, 2011) however, the notion that ICTs and technologization bring us closer to the globalization frontier remains a challenge. It seems that we have too much too soon—information and communication networks are spilling over onto the sidewalks where we once took a stroll to admire the

Milky Way on a clear summer's night, and perhaps e-waste from all the technologization contributes to the gloomy clouds that now obscure our sight. So we need to be more critical about the advances of the new technological age before we ride too comfortably on the globalization bandwagon. In particular, we have to examine the effects of technologization and globalization on human life and on the environment and to identify the less positive aspects of technology in this new age. In other words, it is time for a reality check and to bust the myths of increased access and possession of technology leading to an eradication of poverty and to an improvement in our social conditions.

Gurumurthy (2004, p. 9) argues that 'new information and communication technologies (ICTs), especially the Internet, have been seen as ushering in a new age' however not all their outcomes have been positive. This is a message that we hear all the time from developing community contexts but one that often falls through the cracks when ICTs are being bought and sold as magic wands of the new age that promise to bring happiness, prosperity, liberation, and equality for all. And yet, the reality is that impoverished communities around the world cannot find suitable sustenance that is non-bioengineered; they hold low-paying jobs or no jobs at all, and they remain homeless and hungry. The current wave of socio-political turbulence and economic strife around the world is testimony to the fact that technologization and globalization did not bring the prosperity, equity and liberation from poverty that was promised. From New York and Boston in the United States of America and from Toronto in Canada to Tunisia, Egypt and China, we are witnessing the largest mass movement of protest against global poverty that is the product of corporate greed and corrupt governments. Social inequities, income disparity and rising unemployment resulting from globalization and technologization is blamed for the frustrations of the people and the uprisings around the world. Evidence of this is found in Flavelle's (2011) article in The Star citing the Wall Street 'Occupy Protest Movement' that claims to speak 'for those left behind economically.' Boute (2011) reports in the Boston Globe that in the Boston region alone 'wealth has become increasingly concentrated over the past three decades. What once was a gap between the haves and have-nots is now a chasm, leaving more families than ever unable to make ends meet.' She also reveals the effects of globalization on the immigrant populations (supporting our contention that developing communities also exist within the developed community context) in Boston who live on the poverty line. Boudreau (2011) reports in the San Jose Mercury News that Beijing as a 'capital city contains some of the world's greatest disparities between the haves and have-nots'. Ferrer and Osama (2011) report that the uprisings and the protests among the developing communities in Egypt, Tunisia, Yemen, Jordan, Libya and Syria known in the media as the 'Arab Spring' can also be attributed to the 'corruption, corporate and political greed and the gap between the haves and the have nots.'

One thing is certain, technologization and globalization has made it possible for significant socio-economic world trends and political movements to collide and to collude in ways that would not have otherwise been possible or imaginable. Evidence of this is found in the use of a wide range of technologies to communicate the political strife and upheaval (for example, the Arab Spring), mass protest movements like the Occupy Movement, and the financial crises (The US Great Recession of 2008 and the current Eurozone crisies) among developed and developing communities. History is being written and rewritten from alternate perspectives as developing communities are rising in protest and are speaking against the dominance of the international development paradigm that has muted them for so long. At the same time, poor communities among the developed nations are also joining the protests out of frustration at being hungry and homeless.Toyama (2010) contends that ' the challenge of international development is that, whatever the potential of poor communities, well-intentioned capability is in scarce supply and technology cannot make up for its deficiency.' We must endeavour to increase capability and to build capacity among those who will write their own histories and who will together shape their collective destinies.

The Western notions of development under guise of technologization and globalization are being contested by developing communities within and outside the (formerly labeled) First World contexts. We are also witnessing a time when the world's greatest democracies are on their political edge because they have exploited the less fortunate in the name of democracy, globalization and technological advancement based on empty promises of uplifting their socio-economic well being.

In the next section, the hegemonic language of international development is reviewed and clarified.

REVISITING THE HEGEMONIC LANGUAGE OF INTERNATIONAL DEVELOPMENT

International development over the past century has subscribed to various labels and terms which were given currency by the dominant viewpoints of Western scholars and researchers. This hegemonic language of international development has been contested; however, it remains on the periphery and therefore it is revisited in this chapter with a view to revitalize the debate with renewed calls for alternatives. Various labels and terms have been imposed by Western scholars to describe the socio-economic and political dichotomy around the globe and these will be briefly reviewed in this section. The authors subscribe to the view that there exist developing and developed communities around the world who may no longer be demarcated by geographical boundaries and that developing communities also exist within a developed community context. Generally, *developed communities* are characterized by their socio-economic, cultural, and political power and status, whereas *developing communities* are characterized by low socio-economic status, illiteracy levels, high level of unemployment, social inequities, lack of and inadequate access to education and health, for example. Other factors that exacerbate the inequities of developing communities are race, culture, nationality, age and gender, for example.

The dichotomized world, restructured and reorganized according to Western perspectives of scholars and researchers (McMichael, 2004; Roberts & Hite, 2000; Rogers, 1995) over the past century, continues to be our point of reference when we refer to those who are more privileged by their economic status and power and those who are not. Various terms have been proposed, digested, and regurgitated over past decades. Among these terms are *developed* and *underdeveloped*, *Third World* and *First World*, the *core* and *periphery*, the *North* and the *South*, the *undeveloped South*, and the *rich* and the *poor* countries. International development must move past the categorization of world communities according to Western norms. We are entering an era in which developed and developing communities are empowered to act on their conscience. Their collective actions to demand social change that is sustainable and just is evident in the Arab Spring and the Occupy Movement and these movements are beginning to demand that the injustices of modernity and technologization be redressed. The socio-economic and political tensions that have given rise to the global unrest have their roots in the old paradigm of international development.

Socioeconomic and Political Tension: Past and Present

In whatever shape and form the current world order has been and is being geographically reorganized and reordered by scholars and researchers from a diverse range of historical contexts, the socio-economic and political tension is visible and constant. The socio-economic and political tension of the past seven decades starting with the Bretton Woods project (McMichael, 2004, p. 43) in the 1940s is alive and well in the present. This tension situates the ongoing bonded relationship among developing and developed communities.

Nearly a century after Bretton Woods, the world is dichotomized on the basis of wealth and of access to and ownership of commodities. The gap between those who possess technologies and those who do not, for example, has not been bridged in the coming of this new age of information and communication technology. Toyoma (2010) claims that 'in the developed world, there is a tendency to see the Internet and other technologies as necessarily additive, inherent contributors of positive value' however ' technology has positive effects only to the extent that people are willing and able to use it positively.' In fact, the gap between the rich and the poor has become widened because of the cost of ICTs; the continued exploitation of developing communities to provide 'cheap labor' to produce those commodities ('globalization has weakened the lowest earners' bargaining power as their jobs are outsourced to cheaper countries' as cited in Flavelle, 2011); and the ongoing colonization, imperialism, modernization, industrialization, and globalization, which all contribute to 'bonded development'. *Bonded development* refers to a form of existence where developing communities (the poor and the starving populations of the world) remain in bondage to their masters in one form or another. Bretton Woods, the old paradigm of development that was exported and imposed, the Great Recession of 2008 in North America, the Occupy Movement and the 'Arab Spring' are examples of such bondage.

This bondage was skillfully engineered and calculated. McMichael's (2004, p. 129) reference to the 'debt regime' or 'global governance, in which individual national policies were subjected to coordinated, rule-based procedures that strengthened the grip of the global political economy' is an apt description of bonded development that holds the developing world hostage to the demands and needs of the developed world or the former First World. The interdependence of developing communities and the less privileged on the developed communities of the world in the 21st century continues to dominate the current world order. McMichael (p. 117) claims that the development agenda was reframed as the globalization project and the World Bank and the IMF 'imposed new loan-rescheduling conditions on indebted states'. Interestingly enough, Truman's message of goodwill and social justice in his 1949 proclamation with an emphasis on the non-exploitation 'for foreign profit' and a vision and commitment to 'democratic fair dealing' (cited in McMichael, 2004, p. 22) did not filter through the thick fog of economic greed in the West. McMichael (2004, p. 149) further claims that the 'demise of the Third World' saw two emerging trends: 'further polarization of wealth and growth rates within the Third World' and 'the consolidation of the organizational features of the global economy, with the lending institutions adopting a powerful trusteeship role in the debtor nations in the 1980s'. The Great Recession and financial crises of 2008 and the current Eurozone issues of 2011 attest to the economic predicament of the West however, as noted by Nayyar (2011), intricately woven in that predicament is the plight of developing communities worldwide. The destinies of developed and developing communities have become bound in complex ways in the global web of deceit, corruption and corporate greed.

Clearly, the foregoing discussion demonstrates that the new era of advanced technologization brings with it new challenges.

THE INNOVATION DIVIDE

Whereas developing communities try to grapple with the digital divide, a new divide is approaching: the innovation divide. ICT can bring about efficiency and can serve as a corner stone to innovate. Defined as 'the process of turning opportunity into new ideas and of putting these into widely used practice' (Lin & Ho, 2007, p. 3), innovation moved beyond mere efficiency gains to wealth generation and international competitiveness as players could reap revenues for their sale of the innovations that they create. Innovation therefore has commercial value to creators as inventions are commercialized for a price. However, the globalization of technology as commodity has given rise to issues such as online or software piracy or 'stealing' of innovations and the infringement of copyright. Current proposals to enact federal legislation in the USA (PIPA and SOPA) and in Europe (ACTA) to protect intellectual property rights and to fight piracy (McCullagh, D. and Mills, E., 2012; Mills, E. 2012) are being contested. For instance, in the race toward green innovations such as solar energy and electric cars (Tsai, Yifu & Kurekova, 2009), key questions emerge. Who owns the intellectual property? Who is the creator? Who makes the revenue and who pays? The nations that produce the most effective green innovations, such as solar energy, would foster not only energy security but also revenues internationally given exports of these innovations. The innovation divide between innovators and adopters of technology mirrors the divide between sellers and buyers, and ultimately that distinction between the rich and the poor. Increasingly catch-up policies in emerging economies such as China and India are moving beyond digitalization toward investment in innovation. Science, technology, and creativity are key to the new era in a global economy increasingly being characterized by innovation for wealth creation and international competitiveness.

REDRESSING THE INJUSTICES OF MODERNITY

Innovation should be complementary rather than an alternative investment to fundamental areas including food, health, and wellness. For instance, governments in developing communities with agrarian roots entrenched in colonial plantation histories and slave trades may be tempted to depart quickly from agriculture given the promise of technology for a more developed future. However, food security is necessary as food is essential for human life. Innovation can be a key ingredient in enabling the achievement of goals such as food and energy security, environmental sustainability, health, and wellness. Innovation policies should be aligned to these pertinent goals and holistic coherent investment made so that innovation does not come at the expense of healthy, strong, sustainable communities.

Redressing the injustices of modernity requires the revitalization of a social consciousness that invokes socially just frameworks to uplift the quality of life for developing communities within and across developed and developing world contexts. This new era should herald a time when wealth is redistributed to fill the empty mouths of babies; when exploitation of women and children in sweatshops around the world is monitored and removed; when global corporations begin to use their social responsibility budgets for sustainable development; and when respect and dignity of human life is restored. It is time to repay the debt to humanity and to ensure that hunger and poverty are eliminated. It is time to approach the diffusion of innovation with an enriched understanding of the important perspectives of the varied cross-section of the world's populations and to foster dignity for all.

REFERENCES

Boute, B. (2011) Report says financial gulf is widening social inequities, housing needs cited in The Boston Globe. Retrieved on December 18, 2011 from http://www.bostonglobe.com/metro/regionals/north/2011/12/18/income-disparity-north-boston-deepens-social-inequities-solidifies-segregation-study-finds/kMaSInb-mLxz6BnoVVs0v7H/story.html

Boudreau, J. (2011) Beijing is a study in contrasts In San Jose Mercury News. Retrieved on December 18, 2011 from http://www.mercurynews.com/china and http://www.mercurynews.com/business/ci_19536546

Clark, D.(2011). Apple fans scramble for new iPhone Retrieved on December 10, 2011 from http://au.finance.yahoo.com/news/Apple-fans-scramble-new-afp-1302947613.html?x=0

Eisenstadt, S. N. (1976). *The changing vision of modernization and development.* In W. Schramm & D. Lerner (Eds.), *Communication and change* (pp. 31–44). Honolulu: University Press of Hawai'i.

Fagerlind, I., & Saha, L.J. (1989). *Education and national development.* New York: Butterworth-Heinemann.

Ferrer, Dhalia & Osama, Bassem (2011). Egypt and Tunisia on the birthday of the Arab Spring In Ahram Online Retrieved on December, 18, 2011 from http://english.ahram.org.eg/~/NewsContent/2/8/29592/World/Region/Egypt-and-Tunisia-on-the-birthday-of-the-Arab-Spri.aspx

Flavelle, Dana (2011) Why the gap between rich and poor in Canada keeps growing In The Star Retrieved on December 14, 2011 from http://www.thestar.com/business/article/1097055—why-the-gap-between-rich-and-poor-in-canada-keeps-growing?bn=1

Ganapati, P. (2009) Has Research In Motion's BlackBerry Lost Its Edge? Retrieved on December 9, 2011 from http://www.wired.com/gadgetlab

Gurumurthy, A. (2004). *Gender and ICTs: Overview report.* Brighton, UK: Institute of Development Studies, BRIDGE Publications. Retrieved May 16, 2010, from http://www.bridge.ids.ac.uk/reports/cep-icts-or.pdf

Hartley, M. (2011). RIM confidence drops as blackberry outage stretches on Retrieved on December 11, 2011 from http://business.financialpost.com/2011/10/12/rim-confidence-drops-as-blackberry-outage-stretches-on/

Lerner, D. (1958). *The passing of traditional society: Modernizing the Middle East.* New York: Free Press.

Lin, C. Y., & Ho, Y. H. (2007). Technological innovation for China's logistics industry. *Journal of Technology Management & Innovation, 2*(4), 1–19.

McCullagh, D. and Mills, E. (2012) Protests lead to weakening support for Protect IP, SOPA Retrieved on January 27, 2012 from http://news.cnet.com/8301-31921_3-57361237-281/protests-lead-to-weakening-support-for-protect-ip-sopa/?tag=mncol;txt

McMichael, P. (2004). *Development and social change a global perspective* (3rd ed.). Thousand Oaks, CA: Pine Forge Press.

Melkote, S. R. (1991). *Communication for development in the Third World: Theory and practice.* New Delhi, India: Sage.

Mills, E. (2012). Anonymous takes aim over Europe's SOPA Retrieved on January 27, 2012 from http://news.cnet.com/8301-27080_3-57367837-245/anonymous-takes-aim-over-europes-sopa/?tag=mncol;posts

Mody, B. (1991). *Designing messages for development communication: An audience based-participation approach.* New Delhi, India: Sage.

Mosco, V., & Schiller, D. (Eds.). (2001). *Continental disorder? Integrating North America for cyber capitalism.* Lanham, MD: Rowman & Littlefield.

Mowlana, H., & Wilson, L. (1988). *Communication technology and development* (Reports and Papers on Mass Communication, No. 10). Paris: UNESCO.

Nayyar, D. (2011). The Financial Crisis, the Great Recession and the Developing *World Global Policy* Volume 2 Issue 1 January 2011 pp. 20–32 London School of Economics and Political Science and John Wiley & Sons Ltd.

Roberts, T., & Hite, A. (Eds.). (2000). *From modernization to globalization: Perspectives on development and social change.* Oxford, UK: Blackwell.

Rogers, E. M. (1969). *Modernization among peasants.* New York: Holt, Rinehart & Winston.

Rogers, E. M. (1976). Communication and development: The passing of the dominant paradigm. *Communication Research, 3,* 121–133.

Rogers, E. M. (1986). *Computer technology: The new media in society.* New York: Free Press.

Rogers, E. M. (1995). *Diffusion of innovations* (4th ed.). New York: Free Press.

Schramm, W. (1964). *Mass media and national development: The role of information in the developing countries.* Stanford, CA: Stanford University Press.

Stover, W. J. (1984). *Information technology in the Third World: Can IT lead to a humane national development?* Boulder, CO: Westview Press.

Toyama, Kentaro. (2010). Can technology end poverty? Boston Review. Retrieved on December 18, 2011 from http://bostonreview.net/BR35.6/toyama.php

Tsai, Y., Yifu, J., & Kurekova, L. (2009), Innovative R&D and optimal investment under uncertainty in high-tech industries: An implication for emerging economies, *Research Policy,* 38(8), 1388–1395.

Wortham, J. (2011). Most young adults in U.S now own Smartphones, survey says Retrieved on December 11, 2011 from http://bits.blogs.nytimes.com/2011/11/03/most-young-americans-now-own-smartphones-survey-says/#more-78155

2   Reframing the Diffusion of Innovations and International Development Within a Socially Responsible, Just, and Sustainable Development Perspective

Fay Patel

INTRODUCTION

The diffusion of innovations and international development literature of the past 70 years illustrates that the dominant paradigm (Lerner, 1958; McMichael, 2004; Rogers, 1995; Schramm, 1964) has aligned with economic development and emphasized economic growth as the key focus. What has never been clearly articulated, except by critics of the traditional paradigm, is that it was the economic growth and development of the First World that remained the priority on the world agenda. During the period after the war in the 1940s, the world was divided according to the political and economic aspirations of Western nations. McMichael (2004, p. 21) summarizes the division of the three worlds thus: the First World was grouped as the West and Japan on the basis of its economic power and capitalist regime; the Second World was the socialist group of countries referred to as the Soviet bloc, and it included the former Russian republic and China; and the Third World was the group of countries that did not align with the First and Second Worlds. In the traditional approach, development and progress were equated with economic well-being. Particularly, the focus of diffusion of innovations and international development research and implementation between the early 1940s and the late 1990s remained deeply embedded in variations of the Western-centric model. In this model, Western countries represented civilized society and economic health and prosperity.

Developing communities were enticed in various ways to achieve the same level of economic prosperity as the West, to imitate Western socio-cultural values, and to succumb to Western economic standards and practices. McMichael (2004, p. 23) asserts that 'development was simultaneously the restoration of a capitalist world market to sustain First World wealth, through access to strategic natural resources in the ex-colonial world , and the opportunity for Third World countries to emulate First World civilization and living standards'. Much of the enticement was through covert operations cleverly crafted through projects such as Bretton Woods, which celebrated its fiftieth anniversary in 1994. Over the past 50 years, the Bretton Woods project has continued to dominate the central world stage in manipulating economic trends and is alive and well, as is evident through the role of key players such as the International Monetary Fund (IMF) and the World Bank 'in international economic interdependence and globalization of economic activity', according to Helleiner (1996, pp. 17–18). Morales–Gomez (1995, p.6) assert that the 'equity, quality, and relevance of existing economic, political and social systems, and processes and opportunities' are being radically altered by globalization.

According to Alkire and Deneulin (2009, p.3), the term *development* 'is ambiguous and value laden' and is interpreted differently in different contexts (for example, material prosperity, liberation, neocolonialism and personal social and spiritual progress). As a result of these varied interpretations 'development processes use and manage natural resources to satisfy human needs and improve people's quality of life' and development agencies regard 'economic growth and productive investment' as a the major concern. From a Western-centric perspective, economic growth and the production and consumption of goods were seen as the end goal for both the developed community and the developing community. For instance, a developed community benefited from the export of machinery and technology, and later, of labor, and it was assumed that developing communities benefited from the import of machinery and technology as well as the provision of labor in the form of sweatshops. Western nations have continued for over half a century to export their innovations and development agendas to developing communities through various educational, agricultural, and technological advancement initiatives and economic aid, for example. The missing link in these innovation diffusion and international development initiatives was human development and a socially responsible, just, and sustainable development perspective.

Human development in this chapter is described as the development of the skills, knowledge, and capacity of humans within any socio-economic and political development context and particularly, it comprises considerations that affect the well-being of human beings prior to, during, and after the phase of socio-economic and political development. *Social responsibility* embraces the principle of individual and collective care taken and given to all aspects of a person's or community's well-being during the design, implementation, and post-implementation phase of development. *Social justice* is a virtue of a person's interactions with another, and it is also regarded as an attribute of individual and institutional commitment to fair treatment of all people. In this chapter, the basic claim of an egalitarian stream of justice is favored as noted by Robeyns (2009, p. 102), in which. 'people are equals in a moral sense: each person should be seen to be of equal worth'. Another term that is also difficult to define is *sustainable development*. It is used frequently in diverse ways to describe various forms and understandings of sustained growth and development. Again, for purposes of common understanding in this chapter, sustainable development will refer to the human- and resource-sensitive approach to development so that human and natural resources are not exploited and manipulated in a way that is disadvantageous to the quality of human life of a community, in the present and the future. Particularly, *sustainable development ethics* refers to considerations of social responsibility and justice within and across a diverse range of technological, industrial, agricultural, socio-economic, and political investment and advancement in a developing and a developed community context.

This chapter makes brief reference to the historical context of traditional models, explores the deficiencies and biases of the older models, advocates a people-oriented perspective and offers proposals for future negotiations in the innovation diffusion and international development arena. Discussion will focus on human development and, particularly, in advocating for a perspective that embraces social responsibility, justice, and sustainability. The chapter will identify various appeals over the decades for a human development perspective and renew the debate so that current and future generations of innovation diffusion and international development practitioners will commit to improving the quality of life among developing and developed communities.

HISTORICAL CONTEXT AND TRADITIONAL MODELS

Historical contexts and traditional models leaned heavily toward narrow Western-centric models of innovation diffusion and international development that resembled the past enslavement of human capital within developing community contexts in exchange for the economic well-being and prosperity of developed communities. A brief review of the historical context and traditional models of the diffusion of innovations and international development illustrates that emphasis was placed on material comforts, social status, and wealth accumulation. These approaches did not consider the impact of the innovations on the people as the recipients of the development initiatives and the ones whose lives would be shaped directly and indirectly by the development interventions. In this way, older models of innovation diffusion and international development erased the significance of the human component and completely obliterated the lived experience and indigenous knowledge of whole communities in developing contexts. And yet, in the 1990s, several United Nations Development Programme (UNDP) Reports and much of the literature of the International Development Research Centre (IDRC) focused on human development as an important consideration in international development. For example, the 1994 Report on Human Development (UNDP, 1994, p. 4) stated that 'a new development paradigm is needed that puts people at the centre of development, regards economic growth as a means and not an end, protects the life opportunities of future generations as well as present generations, and respects the natural systems of which all life depends'.

The focus on social and human development is not a new perspective but rather a renewed call to reposition the traditional approaches to development and the international development discourse . Morales-Gomez (1995) noted that traditional approaches to development were not necessarily meeting the needs of diverse regions around the world in the 1990s. According to him (p.1), 'in the mid-1990s, most Latin American countries [were] repositioning themselves on a changing world stage while attempting to build a new model of development relevant to the region'. Morales-Gomez advocated the need for a human development perspective to development and supported the UNDP Reports and initiatives to raise consciousness about human development. Referring to the UNDP Human Development Reports in an online marketing announcement of their new publication on human development and capacity Deneulin and Shahani (n.d., http://hdr.undp.org/en/humandev/learnmore/title,18966,en.html) claim that the Reports carried a simple message that development was 'about giving people the opportunities to live lives they value, and about enabling them to become actors in their own destinies'. However, it seems that although the messages were simple and clear, the social responsibility to carry the portfolios for human development on a global scale were not clearly defined, identified, or monitored.

DEFICIENCIES AND BIASES OF TRADITIONAL APPROACHES

The export of innovations and development packages often resulted in negative perceptions of the West and, particularly, a deep resentment that indigenous knowledge, values, and voices were devalued and dismissed as significant contributions and agents of change and knowledge transfer. These sentiments resonate throughout the alternate literature that emerges from the developing community context through reports of non-government agencies, presentations of the UNDP, and through various other resources from agencies such as the Canadian IDRC.

Traditional approaches have been driven from colonial, imperial, and cultural deficit perspectives. Colonial perspectives suggest a missionary approach to convert developing communities to a more civil way of life and are based on the belief that 'other' communities need to be educated, modernized, and civilized. In keeping with a charitable and divine intervention perspective, aid in the form of funding, food, and physical infrastructures like schools and child care centers were offered by different agencies, organizations, and corporations. Much of this aid was given as one-time hand-outs and/or piecemeal initiatives arising out of the corporate social responsibility budgets of mainly large global corporations. According to Spero (2010), corporations like Ford, Carnegie and Rockefeller participated in an international philanthropic movement to improve the condition of society. For example, corporate social responsibility budgets of the Kellogg Foundation and the Ford Foundation in the 1980s provided food, infrastructure ('bricks and mortar'), and other machinery to developing communities in Africa, Asia, and Latin America. This was done with little regard for the consequences of the innovation on the local communities, their indigenous knowledge, or their cultural values.

Cultural deficit models either dismiss or disrespect the socio-economic factors of the recipient communities, their cultural knowledge, and their histories. For example, with reference to a curriculum innovation project in Singapore, Rubdy (2008) claims that the technical aid project innovations are not well received because they are perceived as impositions and lack consultation and culturally appropriate responses to the need of the indigenous cultures. Rubdy asserts that in this project, indigenous practices were devalued and the voices of local practitioners were marginalized and silenced. She advocates for an innovation diffusion model that respects local knowledge and that embraces socio-cultural experiences.

As is evident in this discussion, social responsibility, justice, and sustainability were absent from earlier development models. This absence continues to be noted in the 21st century when the demographics of the global population has shifted and the needs and demands of the global communities beg a more sensitive, culturally appropriate response to uplift the quality of life of developing communities, within and across various geographical boundaries. Within the realm of culturally deficit models, diffusion of innovations principles and practices that were custom-made for the cultural, socio-economic, and political Western contexts have been exported to the developing community in the name of international development. These models operate within an export-import foreign aid mindset when diffusion of innovations is exported to developing communities under the umbrella of international development in the form of foreign aid handouts to developing communities.

Clearly, past innovations and development initiatives did not place people first, and so the human component was absent. Human development did not go hand in hand with economic development and the implementation of innovations across the broad spectrum of educational, agricultural, and technological innovations. People involved in the innovations transfer and who were the recipients of the innovation and those whom the development initiative targeted were not consulted, equipped, involved, or empowered to manage the design and the implementation phase and the consequences of the innovative development. As a result, the

1. Social responsibility of all members of the recipient community to enhance the quality of their common destiny was underplayed;
2. Social responsibility of the innovator and development agent was unaccounted for;
3. Social justice principles of fairness, respect, and dignity in enacting innovative and development design and delivery were ignored; and
4. Sustainability of the innovation and the development initiative was disregarded.

In other words, innovations were exported to developing communities and development was packaged and delivered in a top-down format; the push and shove principles operated as the norm. The cultural values of receiving communities, their indigenous knowledge, and the voices of local communities were absent in the design and implementation of appropriate innovation diffusion processes and development initiatives. The people who received the innovation and to whom 'development was done' were not

1. Provided with opportunities to up skill;
2 Trained in the management of the innovation;
3. Enabled and empowered to engage with the innovation in appropriate ways; or
4. Given an opportunity to build capabilities.

Developing communities were not briefed on how to maintain a level of desired development; as a consequence, in some cases they developed a dependency on the innovators to solve their technical training problems, and in other cases they abandoned the innovation or were left with the aftermath of failed innovation and were regarded as 'failed development' projects.

Diffusion of innovations and international development design and implementation have been biased toward the socio-economic and political agendas and prosperity of Western nations. Little or no importance was placed on the specific socio-economic status, cultural values, beliefs, or historical contexts of the developing communities. The social responsibility of all members of society to contribute toward their common good was absent in the innovations and development models of the last century. So, too, was there a glaring absence of the social justice principles of fairness and equity in the interactions among developed and developing community agencies and in the design and implementation of the innovations and development initiatives. More significantly, there is also a dearth of sustainability as a fundamental principle of innovation diffusion and development practice in the literature. Social responsibility, justice, and sustainability of innovations and development were lacking in the last century, and although developing communities were regarded as the targets of innovation diffusion and development, the human development component remained absent. Peoplecenteredness was not a desired goal of innovation diffusion and international development.

PEOPLE-CENTERED APPROACH TO INNOVATION DIFFUSION AND INTERNATIONAL DEVELOPMENT

The author suggests that the needs of a growing diversity in the global demographics of this new century requires a reframing of diffusion of innovations and international development policies and practices to include social responsibility, justice, and sustainability within a people-centered approach. It is important to respond to the changing socio-political needs and economic crises by identifying a model of diffusion and development that will respect the cultural make-up, socio-economic realities, indigenous knowledge and historical identities of developing communities around the globe, as espoused by Rubdy (2008) and Alkire and Deneulin (2009). Social responsibility, justice, and sustainability are fundamental attributes of diffusion of innovations and development initiatives in the 21st century to ensure that impoverished communities and affluent communities alike will negotiate their respective spaces in a fair and equitable manner.

CONCLUSION

This chapter examined the deficiencies and biases of the traditional models of innovation diffusion and international development and identified ways in which developing communities were grossly affected. The author proposed a more compassionate approach be explored in the future. As noted from the preceding discussion, it is time to put people first (Alkire and Deneulin, p.13) in development goals and to ensure that quality of life is of key importance. Future innovation diffusion and international development initiatives should be committed to a people-centered approach and should embrace the principles of social responsibility, justice, and sustainability. In positioning people at the center of development and innovation diffusion initiatives, we can ensure that they will

1. Have greater agency in their own development;
2. Improve the quality of life for themselves and their communities;
3. Negotiate their relationships with their environment;
4. Sustain their growth and development on the basis of their community-based value and belief systems;
5. Embed commitment to social responsibility and justice in all aspects of their development; and
6. Reflect upon and review the consequences of the innovation on their individual and collective destinies.

Our histories may define who we are as individuals however we are bound by our collective destinies. Deneulin & Shahani (2009, p. 300) assert that 'the human development and capability approach is about social transformation: enabling people to become agents of their own lives and providing them with the opportunities to live lives they have reason to choose and value'. We must embrace human development as an imperative in international development.

REFERENCES

Alkire, S. and Deneulin, S. (2009) A normative framework for development In *An introduction to the human development and capability approach: Freedom and agency*. London: Earthscan; Ottawa: IDRC. pp. 3–13. Retrieved June 12, 2010, from http://www.idrc.ca/en/ev-143029–201–1-DO_TOPIC.html

Deneulin, S., & Shahani, L. (Eds.). (2009). *An introduction to the human development and capability approach: Freedom and agency*. London: Earthscan; Ottawa: IDRC. pp. 300–329. Retrieved June 12, 2010, from http://www.idrc.ca/en/ev-143029–201–1-DO_TOPIC.html

Deneulin, S., & Shahani, L. (Eds.). (n.d.). Retrieved December 9, 2011 from http://hdr.undp.org/en/humandev/learnmore/title,18966,en.html

Helliener, G. K. (1996). Part 1: Overview: The eclipse of the G-7. In R. Culpeper & C. Pestieau (Eds.), *Development and global governance*. Ottawa: IDRC. pp. 30–36 on the PDF and 17–24 on the document. Retrieved December 9, 2011, from http://idl-bnc.idrc.ca/dspace/bitstream/10625/13672/5/104056.pdf

Lerner, D. (1958). *The passing of traditional society: Modernizing the Middle East.* New York: Free Press.

McMichael, P. (2004). *Development and social change: A global perspective* (3rd ed.). Thousand Oaks, CA: Pine Forge Press.

Morales–Gomez, D. (1995) Introduction: Development and Social reform in the Context of Globalization In Morales-Gomez, D., & Mario Torres, A. (Eds.). (1995). *Social policy in a global society: Parallels and lessons from the Canada–Latin America experience.* pp 1–24 Retrieved June 20, 2010, from http://www.idrc.ca/en/ev-9296–201–1-DO_TOPIC.html

Robeyns, I. (2009). Equality and justice. In S. Deneulin & L. Shahani (Eds.), *An introduction to the human development and capability approach: Freedom and agency*. London: Earthscan; Ottawa: IDRC. pp 101–116. Retrieved June 12, 2010, from http://www.idrc.ca/en/ev-143029–201–1-DO_TOPIC.html

Rogers, E. (1995) Diffusion of Innovations (4th Edition) New York: Free Press.

Rubdy, R. (2008). Diffusion of innovation: A plea for indigenous models. *TESL-EJ* 12(3). Retrieved June 12, 2010, from http://tesl-ej.org/ej47/a2.html

Schramm, W. (1964). *Mass media and national development: The role of information in the developing countries*. Stanford, CA: Stanford University Press.

Spero, J.E. (2010) The global role of US Foundations N.Y, USA:The Foundation Center Retrieved on January 20, 2012 from http://foundationcenter.org/gainknowledge/research/pdf/global_role_of_us_foundations.pdf

United Nations Development Programme (UNDP). (1994). *Human development report 1994*. New York: Oxford University Press.

3 Empowering Communities
A Holistic Approach for Innovation

Giselle Rampersad

INTRODUCTION

A holistic approach is required to empower communities by providing a model for diffusing innovation that is relevant to developing contexts. The global economy is being increasingly characterized by innovation with marked differences between those who could innovate and reap revenues from those who are mere adopters of foreign innovations with little reciprocal revenues for innovations that they can create. This capacity to innovate has therefore resulted in disparities and economic divides between developed and developing contexts. The current trend toward innovation not only reflects differences in wealth and power but also constitutes increased complexity given the institutional, network, organizational, and individual factors involved. Consequently, innovation mirrors institutional factors such as research and development (R&D) infrastructure, R&D funding, and a culture to support the innovation process; inter-organizational networks of collaborating partners; organizational factors pertaining to suitable management approaches to foster innovation; and individual considerations focused on creativity and motivation to innovate. Hence, this study provides a multi-level framework for diffusing innovations in developing contexts that addresses these complex dimensions. It draws on best practice from developing contexts, with a particular focus on Asia as well as from developed contexts where relevant. The study aims to empower communities by equipping them with a holistic approach for building and sustaining innovative capacity so that they can reap the rewards for their own innovations.

THE IMPORTANCE OF INNOVATION

Most low-income countries do not participate in global research and development networks and consequently do not reap the benefits that they can generate (Former United Nations Secretary-General Kofi A. Annan, cited in UNCTAD, 2005, p. v).

Innovation is critical not only for the advanced economies but also for developing economies (UNCTAD, 2005). Throughout history, innovation has been crucial for human society in feeding populations, providing water, generating energy, transporting people, and finding cures for diseases. Various stages have been employed to classify countries based on their level of economic development. Beyond the industrialization and technological revolutions, nations are now being divided based on their capacity to innovate. Distinctions have been made between countries that are innovators and those who are mere adopters (WEF, 2006). As globalization may pose a threat to some countries, particularly those less developed, policies that aim solely toward industrialization and efficiency gains and ignore innovation may contribute to the perpetuation of present, and the creation of future, economic divides. Concerted strategies that focus on developing local innovative capacity are important. Increasingly recognized for international competitiveness, wealth creation, and economic development (Furman, Porter, & Stern, 2002), innovation has grown in prominence due to globalization, the permeation of information and communication technologies (ICTs), the intensification of networks between organizations and financial systems, and the redistribution of wealth and power among nations. Failure by a nation to nurture its innovation capability may cause it to fall behind and may exclude it from participation in the innovation-driven global economy that is intensifying. Such nations may end up paying for foreign innovations without obtaining corresponding revenues for their own innovations (Gans & Stern, 2003).

Innovation has become a prominent issue for a growing number of developed and emerging economies. Whereas the developed nations, including Japan, the United States, and Europe, have been the recognized leaders in innovation for decades (Freeman & Hagedoorn, 1994; Hagedoorn, 1996), governments in emerging economies such as India and China have also begun to develop innovation policies as reflected in drives to shift from 'made in China' to 'invented in China'. These emerging economies are competing in the race toward innovation, for example, in relation to sustainable energy solutions (Thavasi & Ramakrishna, 2009; Tsai, Yifu, & Kurekova, 2009). With sustainability attracting attention at the international level, countries who are able to create the 'green gems' of the future, for instance, renewable energy and green cars, in a sustainable and cost-effective manner will reap benefits through export revenue, self-reliance on self-generating energy, and prosperity through the development of lucrative downstream products and services.

Innovation in services is also becoming an important issue. The service sector is the largest exporter and employer internationally (Kleinaltenkamp, 2007). The business community has begun to respond to the trends toward service innovation marked by the formation of the Service Research Innovation Institute (SRII), which involves a number of organizations such as IBM and Microsoft, universities, and research organizations from around the world. Additionally, governments, for instance, in the United Kingdom and Finland, have developed policies to foster service innovation (DTI, 2007). Rather than focusing on cheaply manufactured products, innovation in services increases profit margins as goods manufactured elsewhere can be bundled to provide overall service solutions. Additionally, a significant level of service innovation can also be generated through ICT, for example, through call centers in India and Egypt. Whereas ICT access may be a barrier in certain developing contexts, innovation in ICT services may overcome distance, manufacturing, and logistics hindrances and offer possibilities for innovative solutions for government, health, education, energy, and even manufacturing sectors given the shift from toward service orientation in manufacturing (Jacob & Ulaga, 2008).

In devising progressive innovation policies for developing contexts, the Asian context is of special significance. This region offers useful insights incorporating examples of effective positioning in focused areas rather than diluting innovation efforts, by pursuing all facets of modern innovation systems found in certain countries, for instance in Europe and the United States, that require building on previous economic stages (Dodgson, Mathews, & Kastelle, 2006). Whereas Japan has been recognized as an established innovator, Asia includes more recently recognized innovators such as Singapore, Taiwan, Korea, and China (Dodgson et al., 2006; Kim, 2002; Mani, 2002; Mathews, 2001). Turpin and Krishna (2007) argue that China is among the top three R&D performers fueled by increased R&D investment. China's R&D investment was 74% of Japan investment, 40% of EU and 30% of U.S. R&D investment in 2003. This study would incorporate aspects of the Asian context in developing a useful approach for encouraging innovation in developing contexts.

A HOLISTIC FRAMEWORK FOR INNOVATION

A multi-level approach is useful in developing innovation systems because a large number of channels for innovation exist (Bekkers & Bodas, 2008). Innovation is a complex process that involves institutional, network, organizational, and individual dynamics (Damsgaard & Lyytinen, 1998; Geels, 2002; Genus & Coles, 2008). Consequently, innovation mirrors inter-organizational networks of collaborating partners; institutional factors such as R&D infrastructure, R&D funding, and a culture to support the innovation process; organizational factors pertaining to suitable management approaches to foster innovation; and individual considerations focused on creativity and motivation to innovate. Hence, this study empowers communities with a holistic multi-level framework for diffusing innovations in developing contexts that incorporates these complex dimensions.

Figure 3.1 illustrates the conceptual framework that will be discussed further in the next section.

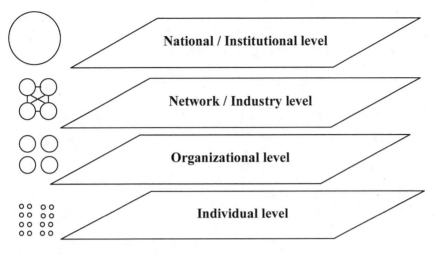

Figure 3.1 Multi-level framework for encouraging innovation.

National/Institutional Level

A number of national-level factors are critical in strategies to encourage innovation, including adequate R&D investment via incentives, R&D funding, infrastructure, and education and skill development in priority areas as well as strategies to generate a conducive innovation culture (Etzkowitz & Brisolla, 1999; Kim, 2002; Mani, 2002).

R&D investment should focus on public expenditure on innovation via grants or through the provision of tax incentives to businesses funding university researchers and investing in the education of scientists. R&D investment has a direct influence on innovation outcomes. For example, in the Asia-Pacific region, Turpin and Krishna (2007) point out that the number of patents filed in the United States by China and the Asia-8 has increased by over 800% between 1990 and 2003, consistent with China's doubling of R&D investment and surpassing the historic benchmark of 1% of gross domestic product (GDP) for R&D in 1996. They indicate that others, such as Indonesia, the Philippines, and Sri Lanka, have faced stagnation with drops in R&D investment and corresponding reductions in economic output.

A favorable culture encompasses both basic necessities, such as acceptable levels of social equity, violence reduction, and political stability, as well as lifestyle enhancements in terms of business and social amenities. In particular, more attention is required at the national level to foster an enabling culture in attracting, motivating, and moreover, retaining creative people who are the main drivers of innovation. As Florida (2002) points out, innovations are created in men of flesh and blood. He argues that the countries that are the best innovators are those which attract and retain creative talent, such as Finland and Sweden, as these have the potential to generate wealth for countries rather than only engaging in expenditure for foreign innovations. He argues that these countries have lifestyle and business amenities favored by the creative class. Entrepreneurial talent is mobile, and although building scientific capacity and providing R&D funding and incentives are all essential, failure to retain creative people will undermine the related R&D initiatives. More recently, countries such as China and Singapore have embarked on initiatives to encourage Diaspora to return and more importantly, to retain their people in building their nations. Those developing countries that ignore the cultural dimension in retaining the creative class will face challenges in sustaining innovation.

Non-economic factors influence emigrants' decision to leave their home country, including violence, racial tensions, and political uncertainty (Kapur & McHale, 2005). Many countries in Latin America and the Caribbean are struggling with unacceptable levels of violence that are indeed hindering their productivity with significant losses of human life that could otherwise be channeled into building successful nations. It is essential that these countries adopt wider policies toward alleviating violence, protecting human rights, and improving social equity, as failure to tackle these issues effectively will lead to the continued outflow of skilled labor and stunted innovation efforts (Kapur & McHale, 2005).

Network/Industry Level

In addition to national considerations, a number of industry or network considerations are also important in developing holistic strategies to foster innovation. Innovation is increasingly occurring in inter-organizational networks given the increasing pace, risks, and costs of innovation (Furman et al., 2002). Networks also facilitate access to wider markets and complementary capabilities and allow organizations to achieve international competitiveness (Kaushik, 2009). Engagement in networks and relationships with international partners would assist developing contexts in their innovation efforts. Innovation theorists have pointed out several key considerations in building effective networks and relationships, including coordination, communications efficiency, trust, and commitment.

Coordination is defined as the extent to which different parties in the relationship work well together to accomplish a collective set of tasks (Mohr, Fisher, & Nevin, 1996; Van de Ven, 1976). Long investigated by management theorists (Fayol, 1949), intra-organizational coordination has traditionally been associated with formalization, hierarchization, and controls (Axelsson & Easton, 1992). Coordination has also been explored in inter-organizational contexts, particularly in distribution networks (Mohr et al., 1996) and more recently in innovation contexts (Moller & Rajala, 2007). In the latter, moderate coordination is favored (Rampersad, Quester, & Troshani, 2009b). Whereas rigid coordination may stifle innovation, some degree of coordination is critical in ensuring that joint innovation goals are achieved (Ojasalo, 2004; Powell, 1990; Williamson, 1991). Given the differences between coordination within organizations and coordination within networks, network researchers have begun to investigate how to best improve coordination within networks. Network theorists have recognized the need for a single authority to coordinate actions beyond the boundaries of an organization as prescribed in traditional management (Ojasalo, 2004; Rampersad, Quester, & Troshani, 2009a). The coordinating mechanism can be in several forms, for example, a committee with representation from all parties or a designated organization. Thus, coordination in networks should be synchronizing rather than overly bureaucratic and should have a single leader to ensure that collaborative innovation goals are achieved given the diversity of the organizations involved such as firms, universities, research organizations, and government agencies.

Communication efficiency has emerged as a relevant concept as the innovation context provides unique challenges surrounding intellectual property; different jargons used by collaborating organizations, which may include researchers or business executives; and the costs of communication, as frequency may not always equate with effectiveness (Rampersad, Quester, & Troshani, 2010). Communication efficiency is defined as communication effectiveness given communication costs. Communication effectiveness includes the transparency, credibility, and codification of communication, whereas communication costs include economic costs and secrecy issues (Moenaert, Caeldries, Lievens, & Wauters, 2000). Communication efficiency is important in achieving innovation outcomes (Rampersad et al., 2010).

Relationship factors such as trust and commitment are also important in the innovation process (Rampersad et al., 2009b). Trust has been recognized for its importance in inter-organizational contexts (Dwyer, Schurr, & Oh, 1987). Benefits of trust include cost reduction from a decreased need for monitoring and oversight; generation of improvements due to an expansion of inter-organizational channels; and decreased innovation development cycles through reduction in bureaucracy (McCutcheon & Stuart, 2000). For more than two decades, relationship marketing and related researchers have examined the nature of trust in inter-organizational contexts (Gefen, Karahanna, & Straub, 2003; Hart & Saunders, 1998; Iacovou, Benbasat, & Dexter, 1995; Nagy, 2006; Williams, 1997). Trust can be conceptualized as the 'willingness to rely on an exchange partner in whom one has confidence' (Moorman, Zaltman, & Deshpande, 1992, p. 315) . Commitment is also fundamental to inter-organizational relationships (Anderson & Weitz, 1992; Morgan & Hunt, 1994; Perry, Cavaye, & Coote, 2002). It can be defined as 'a desire to develop a stable relationship, a willingness to make short-term sacrifices to maintain the relationship, and a confidence in the stability of the relationship' (Anderson & Weitz, 1992, p. 19). Demonstrating commitment and trust to partners is essential for innovation (Rampersad et al., 2009b).

Organizational Level

Within organizations of the network, effective managerial approaches are necessary to foster innovation. These include generating an innovative organizational culture, employing appropriate levels of coordination, integrating the interface between R&D and marketing, using effective rewards, and adopting systems to capture ideas.

The culture of an organization can have an impact on innovation outcomes. An organizational culture is distinctive to one organization, organizational unit, or group and may comprise flexibility, time orientation, market orientation, empowerment, organizational compatibility and experience, motivation, goals, and future orientation on outcomes (Medlin, 2001; Plewa, 2005). An example of an organization with an innovative culture is Google, which is the second most innovative company in the world, according to a survey conducted by *BusinessWeek* (2010). In devising an innovative culture, Google uses eight rigorous and disciplined brainstorming sessions per year with 10 minutes allowed to employees to pitch ideas. It also leads innovation efforts from the top, with the Director of Web Products having open office hours during which employees can talk through ideas. It attracts the best talent due to intellectually stimulating culture and good pay levels and also provides motivation for creative talent by giving all engineers one day per week to develop their own personal projects. Overall, it acts like a venture capitalist and searches for ideas both internally and externally to the company. The case study of Google demonstrates mechanisms to build an innovative organizational culture through brainstorming sessions, leadership by top management, adopting steps to attract and retain talent, and sourcing ideas.

In addition to organizational culture, coordination is also important in achieving innovation outcomes. Steps to facilitate coordination include rerouting reporting lines and creating a physical space for collaboration and teaming people from across the organizational chart. An example of effective coordination can be seen from BMW, which is the 16th most innovative company internationally (*BusinessWeek*, 2008). In developing a new car, BMW relocates the project team's members from engineering, design, production, marketing, purchasing, and finance locations to a Research and Innovation Centre. This close proximity contributes to increasing communication and, in turn, car development. It facilitates face-to-face meetings and reduces conflicts between marketing and engineering/R&D at a late stage. Integration between R&D and marketing is important for innovation (Gupta, Raj, & Wilemon, 1986; Song & Thieme, 2006), as most successful innovations tap into a technological opportunity while also having a market focus.

Rewards are also useful in encouraging innovation. Linking innovation goals to evaluation and promotion criteria is well aligned to achieving innovation strategies. For instance, GE evaluates managers on innovation criteria such as external focus, imagination, and courage. Nokia provides rewards to engineers with a minimum of 10 patents by entry into its 'Club 10' and formal recognition by its chief executive officer (CEO) in an awards ceremony. Similarly, 3M rewards scientists with grants to work on external projects. Another means to encourage innovation is through systems to capture ideas. It is essential that innovations are geared toward customer needs. Some firms hire lead customers or hire designers who observe the use of the product by customers at work or at home. Organizations such as Schlumberger and Lego also use blogs and online communities to source ideas from employees and customers.

Individual Level

At a sub-unit of analysis within the organization, individual factors also affect innovation outcomes. Innovation scholars have reported on the importance of individual champions in the innovation process (Howell, Shea, & Higgins, 2005; Santoro & Chakrabarti, 2002). Given that innovation-focused collaborations between various organizations such as universities and businesses may cross fundamentally different organizational environments and cultures, the skills of individuals to understand and to work in other environments and cultures are crucial (Plewa & Quester, 2008). These skills are likely to be based on both the experience and engagement of the individual. The success of innovation partnerships relies heavily on the individual staff members' engagement, experience, and personal skills. In developing contexts, individuals are also crucial for leadership and fulfilling roles substituting for innovation infrastructure found in developed contexts. Prior experience by these key individuals is important in strengthening relationships and improving innovation success.

Florida (2002) indicates that entrepreneurial talent of individuals is crucial for innovation. In terms of entrepreneurial talent, there are disparities between countries experiencing brain drain compared to those experiencing brain gain. Entrepreneurial talent is defined as highly skilled, knowledge-based workers, including scientists and successful business persons. At the national and organizational levels, steps should be taken to develop, attract, and retain talent.

Kapur and McHale (2005) point out that whereas developed countries engaging in skilled migration to attract the best of global talent due to factors such as aging populations, skilled based development, and international integration of financial and technological sectors, emigration becomes an option rather than a prospect for highly skilled individuals from developing countries. International migration has been a major consequence of globalization and has increased in a linear manner over the past 40 years from 76 million in 1965 to 190 million in 2005 (Taylor, 2006). Despite emigration being a forefront issue to governments of developing countries and international bodies, Lucas (2005) argues that no government anywhere in the world can prevent significant emigration. Although there is a direct economic loss to the home country due to absent talent, they present a progressive view that modern-day Diaspora plays a significant role in improving the reputation of their home countries and in connecting developing countries to opportunities in international commerce and academia based on the networks in which they are embedded. Trans-national networks shape economic development in home countries. Lucas (2005) provides evidence from China where massive investment by Chinese Diaspora has fueled China's economic growth. Whether skilled Diaspora return or remain abroad, they can integrate developing countries with the international community, and they have a tremendous potential to provide skills, ideas, savings, and contracts that they may not have been able to offer if they had remained in their respective countries. Therefore, connection polices aimed at strengthening Diaspora interactions may have a positive impact on the economies of developing countries.

PROPOSALS FOR DEVELOPING CONTEXTS

Holistic solutions for encouraging innovation in developing contexts should address institutional, network, organizational, and individual considerations. At the institutional level, governments can take an active role in financing R&D and infrastructure for innovation; serve as a lead user; establish an information center, department, or ministry with an innovation, science, and technology portfolio; foster an environment of political and economic stability; provide complementary assets; act as a regulator with policy interventions and incentives; invest in education and the development of scientific human resources and foster an environment in conjunction with business involvement with suitable cultural, lifestyle, and business amenities, particularly in technology parks and innovation hubs (Etzkowitz & Brisolla, 1999; Florida, 2002; Kim, 2002; Mani, 2002).

At the network level, adequate coordination is necessary with a single clear leader to ensure that outcomes are achieved and which adopts a synchronizing rather than overly bureaucratic role given the variety of organizations that may be involved (Rampersad et al., 2010). Communication efficiency is also critical with transparency in funding criteria and input of partners, credibility of the process, and codification so that participants understand the involvement of collaborators. It is also important that the communication costs be considered and a system adopted to address intellectual property issues. Relationships between collaborators are also instrumental. Success in small projects can lead to the larger projects with the same partner, in so doing demonstrating commitment and building trust in the relationship.

At the organizational level, it is crucial to engender an innovative organizational culture; adopt appropriate levels of coordination, strengthen the interface between R&D and marketing, use effective rewards, and implement systems to capture ideas.

At the individual level, steps should be taken to motivate and stimulate an interest in innovation through recognition and highlighting success stories; identify champions to lead that are equipped or provided with opportunities to acquire relevant experience; develop, attract, and retain talent; and implement connection policies with Diaspora.

CONCLUSION

By learning from the experiences and findings from studies on developed countries as well as on developing countries that have been experiencing returns from their innovation efforts, strategic implications are offered to increase the rate and effectiveness of technological catch-up by developing countries wishing to embark on or improve such initiatives. Whereas developing countries face a plethora of issues that may hinder innovation, encouraging innovation requires methodological and sustained efforts. This study is intentionally based on a positive and hopeful stance as relevant, and successful examples are indeed present and could be drawn on from developing countries, particularly from Asia (Turpin & Krishna, 2007). These include China (Dodgson et al., 2006), Korea (Kim, 2002), and Taiwan (Mathews, 2001). In each of these cases, political will has been a pivotal factor in sustained efforts. The study offers a multi-level framework to policymakers and managers which incorporate fundamental institutional issues; network considerations, given the increased significance of the network in fostering innovation; managerial approaches within organizations; and individual factors, as innovation ultimately occurs in individuals.

REFERENCES

Anderson, E., & Weitz, B. (1992). The use of pledges to build and sustain commitment in distribution channels. *Journal of Marketing Research, 24*(1), 18–34.

Axelsson, B., & Easton, G. (1992). *Industrial networks: A new view of reality*; London: Routledge.

Bekkers, R., & Bodas, F. I. M. (2008). Analysing knowledge transfer channels between universities and industry: To what degree do sectors also matter? *Research Policy, 37*, 1837–1853.

BusinessWeek. (2010). http://www.businessweek.com/interactive_reports/innovative_companies_2010.htmlRetrieved December 17 2011.

Damsgaard, J., & Lyytinen, K. (1998). Contours of diffusion of electronic data interchange in Finland: Overcoming technological barriers and collaborating to make it happen. *Journal of Strategic Information Systems, 7*(4), 275–297.

Dodgson, M., Mathews, J., & Kastelle, T. (2006). The evolving role of research consortia in East Asia. *Innovation: Management, Policy & Practice, 8*(1), 84–101.

Department of Trade and Industry (DTI). (2007, June). *Innovation in services, 2007* (DTI Occasional Paper No. 9). London, UK: Author.

Dwyer, F. R., Schurr, P. H., & Oh, S. (1987). Developing buyer-seller relationships. *Journal of Marketing, 51*(2), 11–27.

Etzkowitz, H., & Brisolla, S. N. (1999). Failure and success: The fate of industrial policy in Latin America and South East Asia. *Research Policy, 28*(4), 337–445.

Fayol, H. (1949). *General and industrial management* (C. Storrs, Trans.). London: Pitman.

Florida, R. (2002). *The rise of the creative class: And how it's transforming work, leisure, community and everyday life.* New York: Basic Books.

Freeman, C., & Hagedoorn, J. (1994). Catching up or falling behind: Patterns in international interfirm technology partnering. *World Development, 22*, 771–780.

Furman, J. L., Porter, M. E., & Stern, S. (2002). The determinants of national innovative capacity. *Research Policy, 31*, 899–933.

Gans, J., & Stern, S. (2003). Assessing Australia's innovative capacity in the 21st century. Retrieved May 8, 2006, from http://www.ausicom.com/01_cms/details.asp?ID=303

Geels, F. W. (2002). Technological transitions as evolutionary reconfiguration processes: A multi-level perspective and a case-study. *Research Policy, 31*, 1257–1274.

Gefen, D., Karahanna, E., & Straub, D. W. (2003). Trust and TAM in online shopping: An integrated model. *MIS Quarterly, 27*(1), 51–90.

Genus, A., & Coles, A. M. (2008). Rethinking the multi-level perspective of technological transitions. *Research Policy, 37*, 1436–1445.

Gupta, A. K., Raj, S. P., & Wilemon, D. (1986). A model for studying R&D: Marketing interface in the product innovation process. *Journal of Marketing, 50*(2), 7–17.

Hagedoorn, J. (1996). Trends and patterns in strategic technology partnering since the early seventies. *Review of Industrial Organization, 11*, 601–616.

Hart, P. J., & Saunders, C. S. (1998). Emerging electronic partnerships: antecedents and dimensions of EDI use from supplier's perspective. *Journal of Management Information Systems, 14*(4), 87–112.

Howell, J. M., Shea, C. M., & Higgins, C. A. (2005). Champions of product innovations: Defining, developing, and validating a measure of champion behavior. *Journal of Business Venturing, 20*, 641–661.

Iacovou, C., Benbasat, I., & Dexter, A. (1995). Electronic data interchange and small organizations: Adoption and impact of technology. *MIS Quarterly, 19*(4), 465–485.

Jacob, F., & Ulaga, W. (2008). The transition from product to service in business markets: An agenda for academic inquiry. *Industrial Marketing Management, 37*, 247–253.

Kapur, D., & McHale, J. (2005). *Give us your best and brightest: The global hunt for talent and its impact on the developing world.* Washington, DC: Center for Global Development.

Kaushik, A. (2009). Inter-organizational systems in a consumer packaged goods network: Case of Godrej Consumer Products Limited (GCPL). *VISION—The Journal of Business Perspective, 13*(1), 79–96.

Kim, J. (2002). *The South Korean economy: Towards a new explanation of an economic miracle.* Aldershot, UK: Ashgate.

Kleinaltenkamp, M. (2007). New value chains. In O. Plötner & R. E. Spekman (Eds.), *Bringing technology to market* (pp. 47–60). Weinheim, Germany: Wiley.

Lucas, R. E. B. (2005). *International migration and economic development: Lessons from low-income countries.* Cheltenham, UK: Edward Elgar.

Mani, S. (2002). *Government, innovation and technology policy: An international comparative analysis.* Cheltenham, UK: Edward Elgar.

Mathews, J. A. (2001). The origins and dynamics of Taiwan's R&D consortia. *Research Policy, 13*(4), 633–652.

McCutcheon, D., & Stuart, F. I. (2000). Issues in choice of supplier alliance partners. *Journal of Operations Management, 18*(3), 279–302.

Medlin, C. M. (2001). *Relational norms and relationship classes: From independent actors to dyadic interdependence.* Unpublished doctoral thesis, University of Adelaide, Australia.

Moenaert, R. K., Caeldries, F., Lievens, A., & Wauters, E. (2000). Communication flows in international product innovation teams. *Journal of Product Innovation Management, 17*(5), 360–377.

Mohr, J. J., Fisher, R. J., & Nevin, J. R. (1996). Collaborative communication in interfirm relationships: Moderating effects of integration and control. *Journal of Marketing, 60*(3), 103–115.

Moller, K. K., & Rajala, A. (2007). Rise of strategic nets: New modes of value creation. *Industrial Marketing Management, 36*(7), 895–908.

Moorman, C., Zaltman, G., & Deshpande, R. (1992). Relationships between providers and users of market research: The dynamics of trust within and between organizations. *Journal of Marketing Research, 24*(3), 314–328.

Morgan, R. M., & Hunt, S. D. (1994). The commitment-trust theory of relationship marketing. *Journal of Marketing, 58*(3), 20–38.

Nagy, A. (2006). Collaboration and conflict in the electronic integration of supply chains. In *Proceedings of the 39th Hawaii International Conference on System Sciences*, Hawaii.

Ojasalo, J. (2004). Management of innovation networks: Two different approaches. In *Proceedings from the 20th IMP Conference* (pp. 1–26). Copenhagen, Denmark: IMP Group.

Perry, C., Cavaye, A. L. M., & Coote, L. (2002). Technical and social bonds within business-to business relationships. *Journal of Business and Industrial Marketing, 17*(1), 75–88.

Plewa, C. (2005). *Key drivers of university-industry relationships and the impact of organizational culture difference: A dyadic study.* Unpublished manuscript, University of Adelaide.

Plewa, C., & Quester, P. G. (2008). A dyadic study of 'champions' in university-industry relationships. *Asia-Pacific Journal of Marketing and Logistics, 20,* 211–226.

Powell, W. W. (1990). Neither market nor hierarchy: Network forms of organization. *Research in Organizational Behavior, 12,* 295–336.

Rampersad, G., Quester, P., & Troshani, I. (2009a). Developing and evaluating scales to assess innovation networks. *International Journal of Technology Intelligence and Planning, 5*(4), 402–420.

Rampersad, G., Quester, P., & Troshani, I. (2009b). Management of networks involving technology transfer from public to private sector: A conceptual framework. *International Journal of Technology Transfer and Commercialisation, 8*(2/3), 121–141.

Rampersad, G., Quester, P., & Troshani, I. (2010). Managing innovation networks: Exploratory evidence from ICT, biotechnology and nanotechnology networks. *Industrial Marketing Management, 39*(5), 793–805.

Santoro, M., & Chakrabarti, A. K. (2002). Firm size and technology centrality in industry-university interactions. *Research Policy, 31,* 1163–1180.

Song, M., & Thieme, R. J. (2006). A cross-national investigation of the R&D-marketing interface in the product innovation process. *Industrial Marketing Management, 35*(3), 308–322.

Taylor, E. J. (2006). International migration and economic development. *Proceedings from the International Symposium on International Migration and Economic Development*. Population Division, Department of Economic and Social Affairs, United Nations Secretariat. Italy.

Thavasi, V., & Ramakrishna, S. (2009). Asia energy mixes from socio-economic and environmental perspectives. *Energy Policy, 37*(11), 4240–4250.

Tsai, Y., Yifu, J., & Kurekova, L. (2009). Innovative R&D and optimal investment under uncertainty in high-tech industries: An implication for emerging economies. *Research Policy, 38*(8), 1388–1395.

Turpin, T., & Krishna, V. V. (2007). *Science, technology policy and the diffusion of knowledge: Understanding the dynamics of innovation systems in the Asia Pacific*. Northampton, MA: Edward Elgar.

United Nations Conference of Trade and Development (UNCTAD). (2005). World investment report: Transnational corporations and the internationalization of R&D. New York: United Nations.

Van de Ven, A. H. (1976). On the nature, formation, and maintenance of relations among organizations. *Academy of Management Review, 4,* 24–36.

World Economic Forum (WEF). (2006). *Global competitiveness report 2005–2006*. Retrieved June 1, 2006, from www.weforum.org

Williams, T. (1997). Interorganizational information systems: Issues affecting interorganizational cooperation. *Journal of Strategic Information Systems, 6*(3), 231–250.

Williamson, O. E. (1991). Comparative economic organization: The analysis of discrete structural alternatives. *Administrative Science Quarterly, 36*(2), 269–296.

Part II

Innovative Technology
Impact on Developing Communities

Over the past decades, one of the most notable impacts of diffusion of innovations has been in the rapidly growing field of technology across a wide range of industries. One of the most contested and debated area of technology diffusion is the assumption that more communities will be empowered through their use of technologies and that the socio-economic gaps among communities will be eradicated. McLuhan's (1962) claim that 'the medium is the message' has taken on a complexity beyond even his own imagination and his claim that the world will become a 'global village' (McLuhan, 1964) is also remarkable in terms of futuristic foresight and vision. However, with new communication media emerging at an incredible pace over the last decade and the impact that it has on developing and developed communities, it becomes necessary to ask 'which medium' and 'what message' are appropriate in the 21st century and for whom?. Of particular significance is the impact of the ICTs on developing communities.

Various approaches to media diffusion and impacts of the diffusion of innovations are critically reviewed in Part Two of the book. This illustrates the diversity of the impact and also the range of application of media diffusion and its consequences on developing communities. Goorahoo and Sooknanan claim that in Trinidad & Tobago, the hybridization of mainstream and development news as a media impact the socio-economic conditions of its citizenry in a developing context. It is noted that its role as a catalyst for social change cannot be underestimated. Next, Patel analyses the long standing debate about gender equity. She addresses the assumption that women and men will share the virtual space in a fair and reasonably civil manner and finds that current practices indicate that the gendered space on the virtual frontier remains an area of contestation. Sooknanan and Goorahoo approach entertainment-education (E-E) as a critical catalyst in social change and suggest that E-E must not be underestimated because it is a potentially significant mode of diffusion of ideas across in developed and developing communities alike. Goodwin and Susanto investigated the individual acceptance of SMS–based government services and report on the development of a conceptual framework. Findings suggest that attitudes towards usage, behavioural control and social influences contribute to the individual acceptance of SMS-based government services. Mundkur analyses the role of government agents or institutional entrepreneurs in shaping the development of information systems. She argues that an institutional bias towards the design and adoption of the technology is strategically calculated and skilfully imposed.

REFERENCES

McLuhan, M. (1962). *The Gutenberg Galaxy: The Making of Typographic Man* (1st Ed.) Toronto, Canada: Univ. of Toronto Press
McLuhan, M. (1964) *Understanding Media: The Extensions of Man* (1st Ed.) NY, USA: McGraw Hill

4 Hybridizing Mainstream and Development News

A Development Perspective From Trinidad and Tobago

Anil Goorahoo and Prahalad Sooknanan

INTRODUCTION

Development news came into focus in post–World War II on the initiative of the United Nations Educational, Scientific and Cultural Organization (UNESCO) to give governments in under-developed and developing countries the kick-start they needed toward economic and infrastructural development. It was premised on the belief that media could be used to help expedite the process of development, by exposing Third World countries to the experiences of the First World, and simultaneously avoid many of the pitfalls. However, this initiative failed amid severe criticisms, including concerns that development news amounted to no more than government public relations which made media mouthpieces for governments.

A universal definition of *development news* that completely captures its meaning and significance, and which clearly defines what exactly qualifies as development news and what does not, remains elusive. Notwithstanding, there are compelling arguments that have been made for and against development news as well as for and against a mainstream approach to news production. Advocates on both sides of the fence have argued stridently for one and against the other. What has been conspicuously lacking, however, is in-depth analysis of how the two contexts may work simultaneously, to the extent that it is at all possible, within any given media structure, to enhance development efforts in developing countries.

The absence of a hybrid of mainstream and development news may be attributed to a lack of consensus regarding their definitions, particularly the latter. Narinder K. Aggarwala, an Indian-born journalist working for the United Nations Development Programme and who produced one of the more widely accepted definitions of *development news*, concedes that an all-inclusive definition is not easy to provide (Aggarwala, 1979).

DEVELOPMENT NEWS

The concept of development news originated after World War II when some Western European states were weaning themselves from their former colonies. There was considerable debate about how these former colonies could be set on a path of rapid, sustainable economic and political development. This discussion culminated in the New World Information and Communications Order (NWICO)—the corollary to the New World Economic Order (NWEO). Its central philosophy, according to Thussu (1996), was that media could be harnessed to promote social and political development and nation building within a democratic framework. One of its main supporters, Schramm (1964), saw mass media as an ideal vehicle that would transport ideas and models of industrialization and modernization that had already proved successful in developed countries to Third World underdeveloped countries. He posited that the task of the mass media of information and the 'new media' of education is to speed and ease the long, slow, social transformation required for economic development and, in particular, to speed and smooth the task of modernizing human resources behind the national effort.

As it turned out, NWICO is regarded as having failed for a number of reasons but primarily because it ignored the peculiar characteristics and historical experiences of the countries of the Third World. What emerged out of the NWICO experience was the knowledge that mass media did not live up to perceived expectations. Instead, the concept of development journalism was advocated. Thussu (1996) argues that development journalism places emphasis on investigating the processes behind a story rather than merely recording the news event itself.

Thussu's description mirrors that of Aggarwala (1979), who regards development news as a means of critically examining, evaluating, and reporting on the relevance of development projects to national and local needs. It highlights 'the difference between a planned scheme and its actual implementation, and the difference between its impact on people as claimed by government officials and as it actually is' (Aggarwala, 1979, pp. 180–181). Aggarwala's assertion is that the fundamental difference between development news and other forms of news is the news agenda and not the practice. He acknowledges that in treatment, development news is no different from regular news or investigative reporting.

DISTINGUISHING DEVELOPMENT NEWS
FROM MAINSTREAM NEWS

From Aggarwala's description of development news, one can infer that mainstream news—or regular news, as he refers to it—would be news that does not go so far as to critically assess implementation of a planned scheme or its eventual impact on people. Instead, mainstream news would likely limit itself to reporting that the particular event took place. The very term *mainstream* conjures images of something mundane, routine, conformist, generally accepted, and readily available. Its definition, according to the *Revised and Updated Illustrated Oxford Dictionary* (1998), is 'the prevailing trend in opinion'. Generally, mainstream media are perceived as outlets that are in harmony with the prevailing direction of influence in the culture at large. These definitions fit Dickinson's (1996) description of "the 'neutral reporter', content to exercise his/her craft skills in processing officially produced and sanctioned information and passing this on to an audience left to make their own interpretations of the information supplied" (p. 23). This contrasts sharply with the definition of development, given by the *Revised and Updated Illustrated Oxford Dictionary* (1998), as 'a stage of growth or advancement' and which conjures images of excitement, pro-activity, agenda-setting, positive, not readily available, change and evolution. All of these definitions reinforce Thussu's argument that a key characteristic of development journalism is its deliberate and pro-active role as an agent for social change, although he readily admits the role distinguishes development journalism from conventional Western notions of objective reporting. His clear implication, with which Aggarwala concurs, is that there is a direct link between mainstream media and objective reporting, which is regarded as the hallmark of Western journalism. It follows logically, therefore, that if mainstream news is characterized by objective reporting, then development news must not be objective reporting.

Cohen (1963) makes the distinction when he identifies separate conceptions of the reporters' role as 'neutral' or 'participant'. The concept of a neutral reporter refers to a press that serves as an informer whose function is simply to convey a message from its sender to the mass audience. The concept of the participant goes directly to the idea of the media as the fourth estate, in which media represent the interests of the public, is a critic of government, and is an advocate of public policy.

Western opponents to development news have used this advocacy characteristic to undermine its validity as a globally accepted form of journalism and have sought to link it with state propaganda. Critics such as Sussman (1976) see it as a means by which governments control the press under the guise of mobilizing economic growth. These criticisms seem designed to hold up mainstream journalism—preferred for its objective reporting, least we forget—as a core professional value (Carey, 1969; Hetherington, 1985; Janowitz, 1975; Lippmann, 1922; Morrison & Tumber, 1988; Phillips, 1977; Roshco, 1975; Schudson, 1978; Tuchman, 1978; Weaver & Wilhoit, 1996). However, cursory examination of the practice of mainstream journalism would reveal that objectivity, which itself is often linked to reporters' freedom to act independently and with little restrictions, may not be as commonplace as we are led to believe.

It should be noted here that the challenges encountered in mainstream journalism are by no means limited to media within this context. On the contrary, many of these challenges, particularly as they relate to issues of organizational structure and the influence of media owners and powerful clients, are very present in development journalism. This leads Aggarwala (1979) to conclude that in treatment, development news is no different from regular news or investigative reporting because in gathering, preparing, and distributing news, they confront the same kinds of issues. In fact, development journalism and production of development news have a few unique challenges of their own. Chief among them is the issue of public and industry acceptance as a legitimate form of journalism.

It is this issue of credibility that appears to be the major challenge confronting development journalists: the challenge of determining, at a personal level, what they hope to achieve at a professional level and by what means they hope to achieve it. It is, therefore, a key issue of neutrality versus advocacy. In other words, do reporters stick to simply telling a story about an event and the way the event unfolded, presenting only the bare facts and leaving it to the audience to assess those facts, or do they tell a story about the implications, consequences, and potential outcomes of that event, volunteering an interpretation that could lead their audience to draw conclusions in a particular way? If they decide on the latter, what is their motivation or rationale for telling the story? Also, can they surrender objectivity and simultaneously retain goals of fairness and accuracy? Critics of development journalism, such as Sussman (1976), suggest not.

Although the debate is about the credibility of development journalism and development news, a critical issue is the extent to which mainstream journalism is objective and credible. If development journalism is to be criticized for lacking objectivity, it follows that mainstream journalism, which is built on the principle of objective reporting, should meet the criteria for objectivity. However, some advocates of development journalism argue there is no such thing as true objectivity in reporting as there will always be some implicit bias, whether political, personal, or metaphysical, whether intentional or subconscious. Klapper's (1960) study of media effects on mass audiences showed that media operated within a pre-existing structure of social relationships and a particular social and cultural context. A crucial point was that media's ability to influence audiences depended on the life experiences of individual members of the audiences. Similarly, media practitioners, who are both producers and consumers of media output, also operate within pre-existing social structures. Humans are also influenced, in thinking and in conduct, by life experiences and no doubt bring those experiences to bear on their work. In this context, can any individual, news reporter or otherwise, claim to be totally unbiased or neutral with respect to any issue? The difference, therefore, between a biased journalist in mainstream media and a biased journalist in development media has to be how each chooses to treat with his biases.

Notwithstanding, advocates of mainstream journalism continue to claim moral high ground over development journalism, so much so that despite assistance from international bodies such as UNESCO, a number of developmental news organizations, such as Pan African News Agency, Caribbean News Agency, and Organization of Pacific-African News Agencies, have fallen by the wayside. They were never able to completely shed the label of mouthpieces for governments and their agencies. Boyd-Barrett and Thussu (1992) blame their heavy reliance on governments for patronage or revenue and the fact that they were unable to significantly influence the news agendas of their respective regions owing to problems of journalist recruitment and training as well as lack of access to sources.

What all of these challenges demonstrate is that news production—mainstream or development—is hardly a scientific process but that the final news product is often the result of personal judgments, whether on the part of journalists or on the part of the organizations they represent. It is this context which emphasizes Aggarwala's assertion that the fundamental difference between development news and other forms of news is the news agenda and not the practice.

MEDIA IN TRINIDAD AND TOBAGO

Until the end of 1990, there were only two daily newspapers in Trinidad and Tobago (T&T), five radio frequencies, and one solitary television station that was government owned and operated. Two of the five radio frequencies were also owned by the government, and the other three were sister companies to one of the daily newspapers. Among them, these eight media entities employed no more than 50 full-time journalists at any one time, none of whom had formal training in news and journalism.

Starting in 1991, there has been a virtual explosion of media houses (all of them privately owned and operated, mostly radio stations) coming into commercial operation. At the end of the first quarter of 2008, the media landscape in T&T featured 2 open-to-air television stations with 2 more in development, 10 local cable television companies, 3 daily newspapers, 5 weekly newspapers, and 39 radio frequencies. As a condition of their operating licenses, each of the 39 radio stations is required to broadcast regular news updates (most have hourly updates of varying lengths), putting pressure on them to hire news staff.

The inevitable result has been a dramatic, almost overnight, jump in the number of practitioners entering the specialized field of news and journalism and, like their predecessors in the industry, most of today's practitioners in T&T media lack formal training in the discipline. The harsh reality is that T&T has not had a history of training its journalists, and media houses do not (and never did) insist upon formal training as a mandatory qualification for employing journalists.

Practitioners are consequently not fully aware of their roles in and responsibilities toward society. They do not appear to have well-defined ideological perspectives of the social responsibilities of media and there-fore do not appear to have a clear focus on their role as either reporters of hard facts (as per the dominant theory of mainstream journalism) or as advocates for social change and national development (as per the domi-nant theory of developmental journalism). The result is that reporters seem caught between two worlds, perhaps without even realizing it, in which they practice both forms. Interestingly, this has produced an approach to news production that has helped T&T media fulfill their obligations to citizens and simultaneously to inhibit the growth and development of jour-nalism itself.

The failing of this system (of not having trained and qualified journal-ists) was hidden when media numbers were small, but this failing has come to the fore with the advent of a larger number of media houses and more practitioners. The likelihood that mistakes (serious ones at that) would be (and indeed have been) made has increased considerably. The frequency and seriousness of some of these mistakes have resulted in public indiffer-ence toward media and media practitioners, if not to outright suspicion, distrust, and disrespect.

INFLUENCES IN TRINIDAD NEWS PRODUCTION

With a lack of formal training to guide the performance of their duties, reporters in T&T learn their trade on the job, through interaction with senior colleagues and editors. In this way, they are exposed to principles of fairness, objectivity, and unbiased reporting—principles which sometimes remain ambiguous throughout their careers but which some interpret to mean presenting both sides of the story and taking care not to incorporate personal views into the final product.

This kind of 'objective' reporting is the foundation upon which T&T media are built, and their commitment to it was demonstrated when media came out in almost unanimous opposition to a 'Green Paper on Media Reform' that the government published for public comment in 1997. It was widely criticized by all sections of the media, which described the proposals contained within it as an attempt by the ruling party to dictate how media should report government's activities. Some senior editors described it as an unsuccessful attempt to introduce devel-opmental journalism.

Interestingly, despite media's seeming vehement 'opposition' to develop-ment news, there is clear evidence that elements of it have crept into the daily output of news, to the extent that development news is now common-place in local media and plays an important role alongside conventional mainstream reporting of events. This contradiction stems, in part, from the freedom that the local media are guaranteed under their Republican Constitution of 1976.

While rejecting outright any attempt by government or other authority to force development journalism in the production of news, citizens and media insist upon the right of individual media houses to pursue development journalism and to produce development news if they choose to do so, entirely on their own terms and conditions. The widely held belief is that development news ideally should include any story that focuses primarily on improving the welfare of the state and its citizens, regardless of who initiates coverage of that story. Nevertheless, in a democratic free market environment, it is felt that decisions regarding which stories to cover and how they should be covered must always be left to media themselves.

INFLUENCES IN NEWS PRODUCTION— A CULTURE OF PROTEST

Media in T&T have historically used their ability to reach mass audiences, and therefore use whatever influence they enjoy, to lobby for themselves and for citizens. This propensity toward media advocacy helped create today's environment in which media and the reporters employed therein use their power to lobby for the living conditions of citizens to be improved. Whether it is a bridge to be constructed in some rural village or the construction of a new international airport, media in T&T have consistently demonstrated willingness to pressure and, when necessary, embarrass relevant authorities into action.

Despite its seemingly blatant defiance of basic principles of neutrality and unbiased reporting, this tendency is acceptable to the local media and the population they serve. A great deal of the support that media enjoy has to do with citizens' appreciation of journalists' emphasis on the human elements of their stories. The approach, which has found favor with reporters and average citizens, represents a conscious decision among media managers and editors to focus on ordinary poor people and their problems, with a clear intent to force authorities, including the government, to act on improving their lives by addressing their issues.

The unintended effect has been to create a culture of protest, which recognizes that blocking roads and burning tires gets attention and prompts positive action. Wherever there is a bad road, citizens are prepared to protest and invite the media, confident that media will give coverage because it will attract an audience that can empathize with protestors. In this way, media and citizens enjoy a mutual benefit.

Having gotten to this point and keeping the broad definition of development news in mind, it is possible now to suggest that in T&T there exists a state of affairs in which media have managed to integrate both the mainstream and the development approaches into their reporting and production of news. However, recognition of that fact raises a more fundamental issue of 'how' integration of these contrasting forms came about.

IMPLICATIONS OF A BUOYANT ECONOMY

Even with a sympathetic population, one could argue that no media that consistently betray basic tenets of professionalism and journalistic integrity would survive very long because they are bound to raise the ire of advertisers on whom they depend for revenues and therefore suffer the financial consequences. Under normal circumstances that may be arguable, but prevailing circumstances in T&T are anything but normal. Even in the midst of widespread infrastructural decay, poverty, and human suffering that easily lend themselves to media coverage from a development perspective, T&T is blessed with a buoyant economy and all-time high revenue inflows.

The link between the economic buoyancy, expansion of the media, and poor standards in reporting is inescapable. Trinidad and Tobago's very buoyant economy supports and has precipitated this lack of quality in journalism through mind-boggling media expansion. As pointed out earlier, never before has T&T had so many practicing journalists, and the vast majority entered the field during the past decade. During the oil boom of the 1990s to mid 2000s when crude oil prices averaged well over US$100 per barrel, there was more money circulating in the local economy than at any time in its history. Advertisers naturally wanted their messages to get out to consumers who had cash to spend, and advertisers were willing to pay handsomely for their messages to get out, through almost any outlet available.

Consequently, in a country with just over 1.2 million people, there was sufficient advertising revenue to support the existence of 39 radio stations, 2 open-to-air television stations, 10 cable TV stations, 3 daily newspapers, and 5 weekly newspapers. Advertising in the press led to dramatic increases in the size of newspapers from a previous average of 40 pages per issue less than a decade before to a new average in excess of 100 pages. Radio stations were mandated under terms of their licenses to broadcast regular newscasts, and most had hourly updates. In both instances, news staff were required to produce copy to fill spaces around newspaper ads and within radio news updates. This rapid expansion of media, radio in particular, contributed in no small way to a level of unprofessionalism and decline in standards of reporting that was unprecedented in T&T history. The decline is also blamed on the speed with which media had to rush to hire untrained, inexperienced, and uninterested reporters.

The rapid expansion of the number of practicing journalists was never met by any meaningful attempt to train these new recruits. Even now, whatever training is offered is done at a very superficial level, in-house, and is usually conducted by practitioners whose only qualifications are their years of hands-on experience but who are themselves ignorant of many theoretical concepts of reporting and news production. In fact, media owners openly admit there is no reason to invest in training journalists as long as their companies continue to be profitable. Unlike the very early days of media in T&T, today's owners are not necessarily practitioners, and their primary concern is returns on their investments rather than the quality of reporting.

On the basis of all that has been highlighted so far, it would not be unreasonable to conclude that journalism in T&T is in a state of chaos and lacks the most fundamental tenets of objectivity, neutrality, and unbiased reporting. Notwithstanding, media and the public they serve seem satisfied with the news currently being produced. While admitting that media frequently take positions on issues and while acknowledging there is always room for improvement, there is general satisfaction that media always report all sides of every story. Even where they take a particular side on an issue, media largely recognize their responsibility to report the opposing side and to give readers the opportunity to arrive at their own conclusions. Despite being criticized and in spite of all the problems, media in T&T claim success in effectively carrying out their primary mandate of guarding democracy and watching over government's activities.

CONCLUSION

While conventional media theory makes a distinction between mainstream and development approaches to news production, the reality in Trinidad and Tobago is a hybrid approach that manages to integrate both. At the center of this integration is the recognition that development news is concerned, ultimately, with protecting and providing for the welfare of average citizens and that media in T&T are prepared to perform this role by any practical means—paying little or no regard to what practitioners regard as theoretical abstractions proffered by academics or the dichotomy between theory and practice.

This unwitting achievement is noteworthy given the lack of training among practicing journalists in T&T. Even more remarkable is that T&T boasts of a highly educated population whose literacy rate is ranked by the United Nations among the highest in the world. It is more than an anomaly that this highly educated and literate population, which pays significant attention to news and current affairs, should leave the manufacture of their news product to a body of practitioners, the vast majority of whom, although formally schooled, have little or no training in the specialized fields of news, journalism, and media. It means therefore that reporters, in particular, set out to report on stories with no clear theoretical basis on which to cover assignments or approach their reporting. While claiming to adhere to mainstream principles of objectivity, fairness, neutrality and unbiased reporting, reporters often manage to unwittingly combine the two forms so that stories frequently start off as mainstream reporting but invariably incorporate elements of development journalism.

As pointed out earlier, reporters' lack of awareness of these concepts renders them void of the analytical capacity and self-confidence to pursue either approach in a thorough and efficient manner. They lack the ability to separate personal emotions from bare-bone facts and therefore do little justice to mainstream reporting. Simultaneously, they lack the skill and capacity to satisfactorily pursue a development agenda. The inevitable result is an unintended combination of the two approaches which, while often achieving the reporter's goal of highlighting social ills on behalf of affected citizens, flies in the face of acceptable standards of reporting.

What is also revealing is the extent to which clients of media in T&T, namely advertisers, overlook these shortcomings in reporting standards. The economic reality is that as long as consumers have cash in hand, advertisers will always spend to reach them. In the end, media will continue to survive and, in the present circumstances, continue using untrained staff to provide their news content.

Perhaps most significant, however, is the historical, social relationship between the country's media and its citizenry. Media in T&T have traditionally placed the well-being of citizens and the conditions under which they live as an area of priority in their reporting. 'Human interest' stories that expose squalid living conditions or unnecessary hardships that citizens are forced to endure frequently make their way onto the news pages of the print media and are featured prominently. Similarly, in radio and television, these types of stories often appear within the first few minutes of the broadcast—a testament to their importance. Editors readily admit that such stories are featured with the deliberate intention that they should force or embarrass relevant authorities into action aimed at alleviating the suffering of affected communities and citizens. In return, media houses enjoy the benefit of public goodwill and audience share in a fiercely competitive media market.

Media savor this privileged position and have gone the other extreme of development journalism in which development is not seen as a top-down approach that comes from reporting widely on government activities but rather as a bottom-up approach that comes from reporting issues that affect the day-to-day lives of ordinary citizens and that forces government, and its agencies, into action. This practice of development news endorses the fact that there is no 'all-inclusive' definition of the term. Accordingly, development journalism was, and is likely to remain, an essentially contested term given its intervention within the shifting politics and theorization of "development" and "underdeveloped" societies (Servaes *et al.*, 1996; Mohammadi, 1997; Thussu, 2000).

Additionally, a new 'multiplicity/another development' paradigm has been proposed by Servaes (1995) which finds favor with current thinking about development journalism. Cottle (2006) suggests that earlier ideas of development journalism (top-down models with inadequate participatory opportunities, noted by Aggarwala, 1979) are challenged by emerging notions of alternative development paradigms. Alternate development journalism paradigms will embrace 'grassroots' community participation and an integration of diverse cultural perspectives as essential components.

REFERENCES

Aggarwala, N. K. (1979). What is development news? *Journal of Communication*, *29*, 180–181.
Boyd-Barrett, O., & Thussu, D. K. (1992). *Contra-flow in global news*. London: John Libbey/UNESCO.
Carey, J. (1969). The communication revolution and the professional communicator. In P. Halmos (Ed.), *The sociology of mass media communicators* (pp. 23–38). Keele, UK: University of Keele.
Cohen, B. (1963). *The press and foreign policy*. Princeton, NJ: Princeton University Press.
Cottle, S. (2006). *Mediatized conflict*. Reading, UK: Open University Press.
Dickinson, R. (1996). *Media professionals*. Leicester, UK: University of Leicester, Centre for Mass Communication Research. .
Hetherington, A. (1985). *News, newspapers and television*. London: Macmillan.
Janowitz, M. (1975). Professional models in journalism: The gatekeeper and advocate. *Journalism Quarterly*, *52*(4), 618–626.
Klapper, J. (1960). *The effects of mass communication*. New York: Free Press.
Lippmann, W. (1922). *Public opinion*. New York: Harcourt Brace.
Mohammadi, A. (1997). *International communication and globalization*. London: Sage.
Morrison, D., & Tumber, H. (1988). *Journalists at war*. London: Sage.
Phillips, E. B. (1977). Approaches to objectivity. In P. M. Hirsch, et al. (Eds.), *Strategies for communication research*. Beverly Hills, CA: Sage.
Revised and updated illustrated Oxford dictionary. (1998). Oxford, UK: Oxford University Press.
Roshco, B. (1975). *Newsmaking*. Chicago: University of Chicago Press.
Schramm, W. (1964). *Mass media and national development*. Stanford, CA: Stanford University Press.
Schudson, M. (1978). *Discovering the news*. New York: Basic Books.
Servaes, J. (1995). *Media and development: Alternate perspectives*. Leicester, UK: University of Leicester, Centre for Mass Communication Research.
Servaes, J., Jacobson, T. L., & White, S. A. (Eds.). (1996). *Participatory communication for social change*. New Delhi, India: Sage.
Sussman, L. (1976, November). Development journalism: A backward idea whose time has come. *Quadrant*.
Thussu, D. K. (1996). *Development news*. Leicester, UK: University of Leicester, Centre for Mass Communication Research.
Thussu, D. K. (2000). *International communication*. London: Edward Arnold.
Tuchman, G. (1978). *Making news: A study in the construction of reality*. New York: Free Press.
Weaver, D., & Wilhoit, C. G. (1996). *The American journalist*. Bloomington: University of Indiana Press.

5 Diffusing Information and Communication Technology Equitably Across Gendered Spaces in the 21st Century

Renegotiating the Gendered Space

Fay Patel

INTRODUCTION

More than a decade has passed since the Internet and email were first introduced as new information and communication technologies (ICTs) across various organizations around the globe. Corporate, government, and nongovernment organizations and higher education institutions were among a wide range of organizations that adopted Internet and email technology with a curious and welcomed spontaneity. Perceptions of the ease of communication and swifter messaging were particularly regarded as favorable features of the new media. According to Rogers (1995), it is not unusual for many early adopters to be among the 'risk-takers' while the 'laggards' cautiously follow. However, once they assess the merits of the new technology and see that it has endless possibilities for communication and advancement on a number of levels, they adopt it with a passion and an energy that is unsurpassed.

Of course, the attributes of diffusing such a versatile technology that allows asynchronous communication to be successfully achieved around the globe in a multitude of ways has been researched and celebrated repeatedly as is evident from the growing literature. On the other hand, scholars and researchers (e.g., Green & Adam, 2001; Gurumurthy, 2004) have also written extensively about the effect of diverse ICTs on various groups and communities suggesting that gender, race, ethnicity, socioeconomic factors, for example, can influence the diffusion of ICTs and that these factors in turn can also be impacted by the use of ICTs. Scott, Semmens, and Willoughby (2001, p. 14) remind us that 'ICT access is complicated because it is embedded in a range of questions about social institutions, social practices and social networks'. For instance, the diffusion of ICTs can be slow in regions where socio-economic factors control access to the technology, and gender-related social norms may affect the frequency of use of ICTs among men and women. Diffusing information and communication technology equitably across gendered spaces poses a challenge because of the phenomenal growth of the ICTs globally. The term *gendered spaces* refers to the traditionally claimed spaces that were socially constructed and assigned to men and women within and across ethnic, racial, and national boundaries. These traditionally assigned spaces have now become obscure because of the increased mobility of migrants around the world, mix of cultures, and, especially, the less visible trans-national boundaries and borders that once defined the socio-cultural identities of men and women. More importantly, the ICTs' virtual environment has also obliterated geographical and physical borders and boundaries, allowing men and women to glide in and out of their gendered spaces with ease and anonymity. These developments give new meaning and shape to gender access discourse in the new era.

The gender access discourse was a popular research topic in the late 1990s when the ICTs were new, and much research activity is noted around the gender divide in terms of social use, confidence, and dissemination of information and gender differences in communication styles. However, although these ICTs are no longer new, they are reaching some regions and groups (remote and urban) for the first time over a decade later. Whereas some of this discourse is familiar in relation to concerns with gender differences, roles, and access, these concerns are now constructed differently. For example, the issues of access continue to be placed on ICT agendas globally, but according to Green and Adam (2001, p. xiv), access is now viewed as 'a less tangible although still restrictive concept'. They claim that new understandings of ICTs in a gender dimension were emerging in the new century with new emphasis on 'leisure technologies, sense of online identity, and cyber-democracy (p. xiv)'. To this list we can add intellectual property rights, e-governance, virtual gender, e-waste, and gender fair access, keeping in mind that the different wants and needs of communities and contexts drive the discourse in multiple ways. For example, Gurumurthy (2004) suggests that the new discourse within the developing community context focuses on the equitable diffusion of ICTs across gendered spaces.

This chapter presents a brief historical overview of the Internet and email ICTs over the past decade. Terminology is clarified with the context of the discussion. Next, issues related to ICT use, online communication norms, information dissemination, and access are reviewed in the discussion, which is theoretically framed within the mass communications and Rogers's (1995) diffusion of innovations perspective. Efforts to diffuse these ICTs across gendered spaces is explored and critically assessed within a developed and a developing community context. Particularly, the chapter focuses on issues and challenges arising from efforts to diffuse these ICTs more equitably and reviews notable changes in the new era, if any. Finally, recommendations are presented to diffuse ICTs in ways that enable less privileged communities to access and use them more effectively for their common good and to urge privileged communities to commit to a social responsibility ethic in ensuring that ICT innovations are more equitably diffused.

OVERVIEW OF INTERNET AND EMAIL TECHNOLOGY

The advent of ICTs brought with it a host of challenges and barriers. Contrary to popular belief, access issues to ICTs move far beyond mere technical know-how and familiarity with technology and machines. There are also numerous implications for right of access to ICTs and for what purpose, making the issues around access complex when we throw into the mix the following: rural communities, poverty, women, illiteracy, sociocultural barriers, relevance of information, language of the ICT, and the status of low- or no-income groups. Gurumurthy (2004, p. 1) contends that for women and rural communities, particularly in countries of the South, the information revolution has gravely marginalized these populations because of 'the absence of basic infrastructure, high costs of ICT deployment, unfamiliarity with ICTs, dominance of the English language in Internet content and indeed—lack of demonstrated benefit from ICTs to address ground-level development challenges'.

Some of the aforementioned factors have been examined and studied by researchers (Levine & Donitsa-Schmidt, 1998; Zeitlyn, Bex, & David, 1998) over the past decade from a developed community perspective. For example, Levine and Donitsa-Schmidt (1998) examined the relationship of knowledge, attitude, and confidence to computer use, whereas Zeitlyn, Bex, and David (1998) investigated the issue of access and denial to the Internet as part of what they call 'the politics of new communication media' (p. 219). Other researchers (Pearson, 1999) examined the use of the electronic network facility's role in establishing a 'virtual faculty of education' (p. 221), and Savicki, Kelley, and Oesterreich (1999) studied the socio-cultural aspects of face-to-face communication styles among men and women and investigated the transfer of face-to-face gender communication styles to online media such as the Internet and email. Internet and email were already in use for various other purposes during the mid-1900s, but access was restricted to the military and to government sources. It was the extension of access of the Internet and email to the libraries, the universities, and the corporate environment in the 1990s on a global scale that has since amplified the complexity of these media to a whole new level, the complexity of which is growing with alarming speed and to unimagined proportions.

According to Rogers (1995), 'Bitnet and Internet are typical of new communication technologies that are interactive in nature; a kind of interpersonal communication occurs via an electronic communication channel, rather than face-to-face' (p. 315). Further, Rogers (p.316) maintains that ' in the early 1990s, BITNET joined with numerous other networks to from Internet, an electronic network of networks' as cited in a case study by Rogers (1995, p.316) "based on Gurbaxani and on various other sources."

The Internet origins are traced to ARPANET, created and used by the U.S. military from as early as 1969. Internet was first made available to the public in 1983 and by the mid-1990s it became a popular form of interactive new ICT that was used by business corporations, law organizations, libraries, and higher education institutions around the world. The general assumption is that with an increase in ICTs at our disposal, all communities around the world will be able to access information faster and to communicate more easily. The myth is that with more information at our disposal, we will become more informed and empowered to act within reasonable measure upon that information to the benefit of all concerned and for the common good. However, Gurumurthy (2004, p. 13) alerts us to the reality that 'technological invention itself is no guarantee of empowerment. A vast majority of the world's population is still untouched by the Internet'. Her concerns are reviewed and further discussed in this chapter along with those of other researchers and scholars to assess the impact of the ICTs on less privileged communities, including the illiterate, the poor, and those who are restricted by socio-economic status and political economy agendas.

The diffusion of the new ICTs is critically reviewed within Rogers's diffusion of innovations paradigm that was adopted by various U.S. organizations (corporations and government groups) as part of their foreign policy in their zeal to modernize and industrialize the United States, its allies, and the developing world.

DIFFUSION OF INNOVATIONS

Rogers (1995), an advocate of the diffusion of innovations theory, described it as a 'special type of communication, in which messages are about a new idea. The newness of the idea in the message content gives diffusion its special character. The newness means that some degree of uncertainty is involved in diffusion' (p. 6). Furthermore, the diffusion of innovations was referred to as a communication process that 'is concerned with a new idea and messages are exchanged about the new idea. This information exchange takes place between individuals or in units of adoption about a new idea through a channel' (p. 18). Central to this discussion is an examination of how new communication technology is received by men and women globally. Gurumurthy (2004, p. 7) claims that 'unevenness in the diffusion of new ICTs is indeed stark. What is more, diffusion defined in terms of availability of physical infrastructure or connectivity may not capture actual use, because the latter is affected by socio-cultural factors'.

In contextualizing the diffusion of innovations theoretical framework and Rogers's (1986) perspective, it is necessary to comment on the references in Rogers's diffusion of innovations literature to labels such as the First, Second, and Third Worlds and to clarify these labels. Rogers was not the first person to use the labels that delineated the First World as representing the capitalist societies of North America, Western Europe, and Japan; the Second World as the Soviet-influenced countries in Eastern

Europe; and the Third World as the impoverished countries in Africa, Asia, and Latin America. However, these labels have been used and misused over the decades and have been replaced with other preferred labels such as the developed countries (modernized and industrialized economically) and the developing countries (economically unstable and impoverished). Escobar (1999) claims that the Western developed countries were responsible for not only managing and controlling the Third World in a systematic manner but also for creating the 'Third World politically, economically, sociologically, and culturally' (p. 33). Further, he claims that the development discourse and practice 'constitutes one of the most powerful mechanisms for ensuring domination over the Third World today' (p. 33).

More recently, other labels used in international development literature include the North and the South. Gurumurthy (2004, p. 1) expands on the notion of the South and comments on the technological marginalization of the South: 'The countries of the South, particularly rural populations, have to a significant extent been left out of the information revolution'. It is time for us to renew the spirit of contestation of the geographical labeling of the less advantaged communities globally and to find opportunities to redress the disrespect given to less advantaged communities over the past century. For purposes of discussion in this chapter the term *developing community* refers to less privileged communities and *developed community* refers to more privileged communities. With the rapidly increasing mobility of migrants across geographical domains, some of whom remain less advantaged even if they live and work in a developed community, it makes more sense to reject the geographical labels (in the traditional sense) and to adopt a new frame of reference, especially in view of the fact that the ICTs have now placed communities around the world in a virtual reality type of existence.

Moving the discussion forward to capture the essence of the diffusion of ICTs in gendered spaces over the years, it is necessary to revisit the early debates about the relationship between gender and technology.

Diffusing ICTs Across Gendered Spaces and Traditional Gender Role

It is evident from the literature (Haraway, 1991; Herring, 1996; Mowlana, 1995 and Tannen, 1994) that early ICT debates concentrated on diffusion concerns focused on men and women's socially constructed gender roles in the home and in corporate organizations; how social mores and graces were being transferred to virtual spaces; the relationship between gender and online social and business communication behavior; women's access options to the Internet and email; access among men and women within developing communities; and acceptable language of communication in a virtual space A review of current literature over a decade later suggests that some of the same issues remain as themes underlying current research initiatives (Gurumurthy, 2004).

Before examining the relationship between gender and technology, it is important to review the socio-cultural perceptions of gender and traditional gender roles. In diverse cultures, the social mores and norms play a significant function in educating men and women about how to behave in the home and at work. For example, Ojong (2009, p. 201) cites the male dominant role among men in the Zulu culture Kwa-Zulu Natal, South Africa, where men are regarded as superior to women, whereas men in Ghana are expected to provide for the families although women in the Akan culture in Ghana are also encouraged to be assertive and to embrace entrepreneurship. Gurumurthy (2004, p. 5), with reference to communities in the South, claims that 'strategies for addressing unequal gender relations will therefore need to hinge on an understanding of the complex intersections of gender and other social identities'. Further, she claims (p. 5) that there needs to be an ongoing monitoring of how 'gender relations as a dynamic cultural process are being negotiated and contested.' Gender roles clearly demarcate gendered spaces so that men and women know the boundaries of their socio-cultural role expectations and of their roles in the economic sphere. Ojong (2009, p. 204) claims 'that in the past decades, gender spaces have been fixed not fluid' but now these boundaries were being reconstructed. For example, in her transnational study on gendered space among South African and Ghanaian migrants in South Africa, she found that gendered spaces were being contested. Hairdressing, which was formally regarded as a woman's job, was now being occupied by men. The International Labour Organization (*Gender Equality at the Heart of Decent Work*, n.d., p. 4) recognizes that women suffer great hardship in accessing employment and that 'overcoming logistical, economic and cultural barriers to apprenticeships and to secondary and vocational training for young women—especially in non-traditional occupations' remains a grave concern.

Pertinent to this discussion is Ojong's (2009, p. 208) finding that 'gendered spaces become unimportant or insignificant when people are involved in transnational spaces'. Most important of all is the realization that gendered spaces are renegotiated and reconstructed. The Internet and email cross multiple borders and transgress several levels of socio-cultural identity for both men and women but especially for women who may already be disadvantaged in a number of ways. Therefore, it becomes important to renegotiate the gendered spaces and to reconstruct them more equitably in the new era. Gender equality is at the heart of the International Labour Organization's initiatives to enable women and men to enhance their employability and productivity in the global labor market. The *Gender Equality at the Heart of Decent Work* brochure (n.d., p. 7) identifies education and skills development as critical needs to close the gender and technology gap.

The relationship between gender and technology is intricately woven within the construct of technology as culture, as Gurumurthy (2004, p. 4) correctly asserts. It is imperative that we heed Gurumurthy's (p. 5) call to recognize that 'women have multiple identities—for example of class, ethnicity, caste, race, age—and that these interplay with gender to define women's access to technology'. Men and women's behavior in their face-to-face social environment is easily transferred to the virtual environment of the Internet and email. There is no doubt that the gendered spaces of the virtual environment have to be renegotiated, but the question is how to do this in an equitable manner.

OLD CONCERNS IN A NEW ERA

Diffusing ICTs within the gendered spaces of the Internet and email proves challenging because in the virtual spaces of the ICTs, men and women continue to meet on the same unleveled playing field. Anonymity in the virtual environment further impedes progress toward a more balanced gendered space. Some of the existing research in areas of communication suggests that when men and women transport their socio-cultural baggage to the virtual environment, power relations continue to affect their line of communication. Michaelson and Pohl (2001, p. 24) are of the view that 'the internet is a flexible technology that can be shaped by the people who use it'. It is time for men and women to reflect on how they can shape the technology together into a viable proposition for sustainable development for the next generation. The Internet and email has the potential to become the catalyst in establishing a mutually respectful global community that works together for the common good. But that will remain part of the utopian dream, and it is only one of the many new challenges for the new era.

At the same time that the diffusion of ICTs poses new challenges in the new era, there are a number of old concerns that emerge. New challenges include redefining gendered spaces to meet specific needs; reconstructing and negotiating the virtual space as a shared space; equitable distribution of power in designing, implementing, and evaluating the impact of ICTs; establishing a code of virtual respect and dignity; and recognizing that women bring innovative and creative dimensions to the virtual environment. Old concerns remain the same as the last decade: access to ICTs, bridging the gender and the digital divide, creating an impetus for the impoverished masses to transcend their plight, the relationship between power relations and access, reviewing gendered communication protocols, upgrading technical skills, establishing infrastructures, providing funding and human resources, and staying abreast of the information surge.

As the list of old concerns illustrates, a decade and half after the introduction of the Internet and email to the global public, we are still grappling with issues of access and have more questions than we have answers. Mowlana's (1995) observations of more than 15 years ago remain true even today: Fewer people can access the new communication technologies, especially in Third World countries; access to electronic mail further isolates certain categories of people from others; and resource access and new media literacy requires funding and support. Furthermore, Wilkins (1999) argued that 'issues of gender, communication, and development are grounded in global structures and processes of power, which condition access to and acquisition of economic and social resources' (p. 47). Gurumurthy (2004, p. 17) claims that 'the uneven distribution of benefits of ICTs within and between countries, regions, sectors, and socioeconomic groups, signifies the uphill task facing developing countries and disadvantaged groups and sections in society (even in the developed countries)'. According to Gurumurthy (2004), cultural attitudes, poverty, and women's multiple roles are among the socio-cultural factors that obstruct women's access to ICTs in rural communities and particularly in countries in the South. Michaelson and Pohl's (2001, p. 23) representing the North made the observation that 'access is still a problem as long as there is no cheap and simple way to get online and that people who are not male, white, and middle class will have difficulties (to a larger or smaller extent) in accessing the internet'. These are only a selection of examples of how old concerns continue to remain in the forefront of the ICT diffusion discourse in the 21st century.

NOTABLE CHANGES: WHAT'S NEW AND WHAT'S NOT

So what's new? An assessment and critical review of ICT diffusion across gendered spaces in the new era reveals that there is a greater advocacy for a social justice perspective. In other words, the traditional segregated gender roles are no longer being accepted without contestation. It is no longer acceptable that men and women continue to behave, communicate, and approach technology in the traditional way, in which men were seen as 'the controllers of information' and women the submissive users and receivers of that information. Gurumurthy (2004, p. 11) claims that 'more recently, there has been a shift from an emphasis on women solely as objects of information to a focus on women as controllers of information'. This is a positive shift toward sharing the contested gendered space which Gurumurthy (2004) claims women have been doing for a long time. Women's place in shaping policy and practices of ICTs is also becoming more current through conferences and projects. The United Nations Status of Women conference in 2003 and the World Summit on the Information Society in 2003 are examples of advocacy for women's rights to better ICT opportunities. Advocacy groups are calling for gender-sensitive ICT policy, more involvement in writing ICT content, and broader capacity building opportunities and developing a shared vision (Gurumurthy, 2004). The Gender Equality brochure (n.d., p. 4) of the International Labour Organization also advocates for equal opportunity for women and men as a priority in education and skills training.

As noted, some things have changed. However, it is disappointing to also find that many of the old concerns remain part of our ongoing struggle in this new era; for example, provision of greater access to ICTs tops the list. Other concerns highlighted in the literature include closing the gap between those who have access and those who do not, the influence of power relations on diffusion, technology communication training, and online gender communication.

Gurumurthy (2004, p. 3) notes that technology is often viewed as gender neutral but claims that, contrary to this notion, technology is not gender neutral. Technology is culture-based and is subjected to society's influences in relation to issues of access, roles, and responsibilities. Furthermore, socio-cultural norms also determine to what extent men and women use technology, how they use it, for what purpose, and when. According to Gurumurthy (p. 4) 'the gendered approach argues that technology is not neutral, but depends on culture'. Gurumurthy's proposal to view technology as culture (p. 4), and within this context to critically examine technology as gender biased, is an appropriate perspective from which to approach the complexity of technology diffusion across gendered spaces.

Renegotiating gendered spaces suggests that there is a need for women and men to meet somewhere in between to revive their combined energies in a positive way, building on their mutual strengths. Suggestions are offered to engage women and men in an equitable virtual space.

PROPOSALS FOR EQUITABLE DIFFUSION AND ENABLEMENT

The equitable diffusion of ICTs across gendered spaces is a good place to begin the quest for shared virtual space in a new era. It is a long-term goal that requires support and advocacy by a broad range of communities around the globe. Particularly, social responsibility for diffusing ICTs to improve the human condition rests on the shoulders of all global citizens and especially those who have the means (the power, the resources, the funds, and the will) to create a shared space for mutual growth and development that will benefit our future generations so that they will live in harmony and strive for the uplifting of humans and nature side by side.

The following proposals are presented to encourage the creation of a mutually acceptable gendered space. Renegotiation of gendered space is dependent upon the following desirable conditions:

- The provision of education and skills training on the effective implementation of ICTs across a broad range of socio-economic and political fronts is critical in improving technology diffusion and gender relations.
- Establishment of a holistic framework for the education and skills training of women and men on technology use and the sharing of

gender perspectives is an imperative if we are committed to bridging the divide on gender, technology, and Internet use.

- Technology and the new emerging ICTs must be redefined as shared cultural goods as the new currency for a new century.
- Virtual space must be reconstructed as shared space with equal opportunity among women and men for creativity and innovation.
- ICT policy and practice must be established in partnership between women and men in interactive forums.

CONCLUSION

The gender and ICT problem thus seems to be an urgent one; once this new socio-technical reality becomes firmly established, people who fail to fit well within it must either adapt or accept marginalization (Green & Adam, 2001, p. 7). The sad realization is that over a decade after the ICTs have been diffused globally in selected spaces gendered groups (among developing communities and developed communities alike) remain on the margins. However, it is not necessarily true that people have failed to fit well within the technologies, but rather that the technologies have not been diffused in acceptable ways to meet the socio-cultural needs of the women and men who are expected to use them.

A more compassionate approach must replace the 'either adapt or accept marginalization' approach: women and men must have a significant voice in deciding what is acceptable in the gendered space and how they will best negotiate that space respectfully. The virtual culture of the gendered space must be equalized to allow meaningful exchange of ideas. Gurumurthy (2004, p. 46) asserts that 'engendering ICTs is not merely about greater use of ICTs by women. It is about transforming both gender politics and the ICT system'. Innovation diffusion and international development practitioners and agents must seriously attend to these assertions and find ways in which to examine 'women's empowerment in the information society' and to ascertain how 'gender relations as a dynamic cultural process are being negotiated and contested, in relation to the technology environment' (Gurumurthy, 2004, p. 5). It is imperative that mechanisms be established to monitor the virtual gender wars and to transform gender politics. Women must not be burdened with the responsibility of contesting the gendered spaces on the virtual frontier.

The BRIDGE overview report (Gurumurthy, 2004) on gender and ICTs identifies the broad guidelines that have been proposed over time across a diverse range of research projects around the world. Innovation diffusion practitioners and international development facilitators may want to consider these options by seeking creative solutions that promote equity and access The following proposals to engage women and men in shaping their shared virtual spaces are offered as a way forward.

- Conscientize women and men to move beyond awareness to meaningful participation in gender forums so that they may action change
- Enable women and men to design and implement culturally appropriate models of ICT.
- Encourage women to embrace technology more boldly 'as producers of knowlegde'
- Challenge the stereotypical roles and responsibilities in technical software and hardware development by enabling women and men in a cross-section of technical skills and competencies.
- Diversify the usage of ICTs so that more women and men begin to share the physical and virtual spaces to gather, disseminate, and design information.
- Promote the development of content by women that is not only situated within their own cultural knowledge base but content that crosses the gender boundaries.

In their discussion on gender and internet, Van Doorn and Van Zoonen (2009) note that gender and internet studies now demonstrate a shift in emphasis from the 'identity vs social structure dichotomy to the manifold interactions between gender and internet technology paying special attention to their offline/online articulations' (p. 268). They also acknowledge that the contestation and negotiation of gender in virtual space will continue to be renegotiated through existing approaches to gender and the internet on a structural, symbolic and identity level. Van Doorn and Van Zoonen (2009, p. 270) contend that in an era of Web 2.0 'with its non-hierachical mode of content production and dissemination [which] has replaced the top-down structure of the so-called Web 1.0', the question is whether the existing approaches will be adequate in investigating the new developments since Web 2.0 is already 'typified by an increasing number of users producing and sharing their own content.' Perhaps, there is hope yet for the future since new technologies will continue to bring new dimensions to Internet gender politics in the future.

REFERENCES

Escobar, A. (1999). Discourse and power in development: Michel Foucault and the relevance of his work to the Third World. In T. Jacobson & J. Servaes (Eds.), *Theoretical approaches to participatory communication* (pp. 309–336). Creskill, NJ: Hampton Press.

Gender equality at the heart of decent work [Brochure]. (n.d.). Geneva, Switzerland: International Labour Office. Retrieved May 17, 2010, from http://www.ilo.org/wcmsp5/groups/public/—dgreports/—gender/documents/publication/wcms_100840.pdf

Green, E., & Adam, A. (2001). *Virtual gender: Technology, consumption and identity.* London: Routledge.

Gurbaxani,Vijay (1990). Diffusion in Computing Networks: The case of BITNET" Communications of the ACM 33(12) 65–75.

Gurumurthy, A. (2004, September). *Gender and ICTs: Overview report.* Brighton, UK: Institute of Development Studies, BRIDGE Publications. Retrieved May 16, 2010, from http://www.bridge.ids.ac.uk/reports/cep-icts-or.pdf

Haraway, D. (1991). A Cyborg Manifesto: Science, Technology, and Socialist-Feminism in the Late Twentieth Century In *Simians, Cyborgs and Women: The Reinvention of Nature* New York, USA: Routledge pp.149–181.

Herring, S. C. (1996). Bringing familiar baggage to the new frontier: Gender differences in computer-mediated communication. In: V. Vitanza (Ed.), CyberReader (pp. 144–154). Boston: Allyn & Bacon. http://ella.slis.indiana.edu/~herring/cyberreader.1996.pdf.

Levine, T., & Donitsa-Schmidt, S. (1998). Computer use, confidence, attitudes, and knowledge: A causal analysis: Computers in Human Behavior Vol 14(1) Jan 1998, 125–146.

Michaelson, G.& Pohl, M. (2001). Gender in email-based co-operative problem solving. In E. Green & A. Adam (Eds.), *Virtual gender: Technology, consumption and identity* (pp. 23–36). London: Routledge.

Mowlana, H. (1995). The communications paradox: Globalization may be just another word for western cultural dominance. *Bulletin of the Atomic Scientists, 51*(4), 40–46.

Ojong, V. (2009). Gendered spaces: Men in women's places. In K. Naidoo & F. Patel (Eds.), *Working women: Stories of strife, struggle, and survival* (pp. 200–209). New Delhi, India: Sage.

Pearson, J. (1999). Electronic networking in initial teacher education: Is a virtual faculty of education possible? *Computers and Education, 32,* 221–238.

Rogers, E. M. (1986). *Communication technology: The new media in society.* New York: Free Press.

Rogers, E. M. (1995). *Diffusion of innovations* (4th ed.). New York: Free Press.

Savicki, V., Kelley, M., & Oesterrich, E. (1999). Judgments of gender in computer-mediated communication. *Computers in Human Behavior, 15,* 1–10.

Scott, A., Semmens, L., & Willoughby, L. (2001). Women and the Internet: The natural history of a research project. In E. Green & A. Adam (Eds.), *Virtual gender: Technology, consumption and identity* (pp. 3–22). London: Routledge.

Tannen, D. (1994). Gender gap in cyberspace. Newsweek, May 16, 1994. Retrieved on 11 December 2011 from http://www9.georgetown.edu/faculty/tannend/newsweek051694.htm

Van Doorn, N & Van Zoonen, L. (2009). Theorizing gender and the internet: Past, present and future In Chadwick, A. & Howard,P.N. (2009). The Routledge Handbook of Internet Politics New York, USA; Routledge pp. 261–274

Wilkins, K.G. (1999). Development discourse on gender ad communication in strategies for social change *Journal of Communication* Winter 1999 Volume 49, Issue 1 pp. 46–68 March 1999

Wood, P. (2000). *Putting Beijing online: Women working in information and communication technologies: Experiences from the APC Women's Networking Support Programme.* Manila, Philippines: Association for Progressive Communications, Women's Networking Support Programme. Retrieved on 28 March 2011 http://www.apcwomen.org/netsupport/sync/toolkit1.pdf

Zeitlyn, D., Bex, J., & David, M. (1998). Access denied: The politics of new communications media. *Telematics and Informatics, 15,* 219–230.

6 Entertainment-Education and Social Change

Prahalad Sooknanan and Anil Goorahoo

INTRODUCTION

Although the concept of development is shrouded in ambiguity, its goal of facilitating meaningful social change is generally accepted. This view is plausible to the extent that education can play a significant role in bringing about social change. Today, however, education and development are at the crossroads, and attention is focused more on the kind of development desired, the suitability of education, and the specific interests of those in the development process (Sooknanan, 2009). To realize these goals, the focus now is on active participation as a means of empowering individuals to attain education that ensures qualitative change. It is felt that the current trend of education generally benefits those in power, leading to a perpetuation of the status quo. Further, the educational trends of the colonial masters are still mirrored in Third World schools, thus perpetuating the historical pattern of imperialism. On account of this, education succeeds in contributing to the ongoing process of under-development instead of development.

Consequently, liberation theorists, and Freire (1971) in particular, recommend the rejection of the traditional pedagogy where receivers are uncritical and passive. In other words, it is essential to liberate the receiver from mental inertia and penetrate the ideological mist imposed by the elite (Diaz-Bordnave, 1976). According to Thomas (1994), this new awareness or consciousness combined with action is dialectically related, whereby action and reflection are not separate activities but an organic whole whose interplay is the basis for 'conscientization' or liberation of the mind. Similarly, Freire (1971) condemns the paternalistic philosophy of education, which he deems 'banking', 'given', or 'packaged' education intended for passive receivers. Alternatively, he emphasizes the need for exogenous knowledge that calls for critical reflection through authentic participation. This approach requires the joint involvement of both the teacher and the 'taught'. In this way, the teacher awakens the critical faculties of individuals and directs them to their true development needs. A current method that aptly facilitates this revolutionary approach to learning is entertainment-education (E-E).

ENTERTAINMENT-EDUCATION

According to Singhal and Rogers (1999), E-E is essentially a strategy of 'putting an educational idea in an entertainment message in order to achieve behaviour changes' (p. 379). They claim that E-E is also known as *edutainment, infotainment, enter-educate, pro-social entertainment,* and *pro-development entertainment* and has been used for decades in disseminating information. E-E is regarded as a useful method by which the public can be informed about important social issues that impact their lives. It involves a strategy of incorporating educational messages into popular entertainment content—everything from soap operas to sitcoms and reality shows—with a view to raise awareness, increase knowledge, create favorable attitudes, and ultimately motivate people to take socially responsible action in their own lives.

The concept of E-E represents the most recent advance to the seminal theory of diffusion of innovation by Everett Rogers (1995). Owing to the theory's versatility and overwhelming application in numerous studies, Sooknanan (2006) surmises that the diffusion of innovation theory may well be regarded as an innovation in itself. More particularly, the diffusion of innovation framework is not confined to merely studying the spread of new ideas or innovations but is equally applied to understand social change. According to Rogers (1995), diffusion is the process by which an innovation is communicated through certain channels over time among members of a social system. Typically, the diffusion of an innovation is essentially influenced by the interaction of key elements such as the innovation itself, communication channels, time, and the social system. Today, however, the focus is more on the social system and the extent to which innovations can succeed in bringing about behavior changes or what is generally described as social change.

Singhal and Rogers (1999) point out that E-E is not a theory of communication, but rather a strategy that is used to disseminate ideas that are intended to bring about behavioral and social change. This may be a response to the reality that entertainment is making increasing inroads into people's lives. Never before in human history has so much time and emphasis been placed on personal leisure and entertainment, nor has so much entertainment been so readily accessible to so many people for so much of their leisure time (Zillman & Vorderer, 2000). More and more people are integrating leisure, relaxation, and entertainment into their daily routines, to the extent that entertainment is becoming a major feature in business and commerce. 'Not only does the public consume more entertainment, it is becoming a more integral part of people's shopping, travelling, eating, driving, exercising and working experiences' (Singhal & Rogers, 1999). It is a phenomenon which Wolf (1999) calls 'entertainmentization' of the world, in which entertainment products and services represent the fastest growing sector of the global economy.

Notwithstanding, entertainment as a field of inquiry is one which early contributors such as Katz and Foulkes (1962) and Sutton-Smith (1988) believe has been largely neglected by communication scholars, perhaps because it is seen as unimportant and frivolous. The reality, however, according to Singhal and Rogers (1999), is that E-E interventions represent an area of unique and important communication scholarship by providing an opportunity to study mass media as agents of both entertainment and persuasion. Accordingly, they have proposed a five-pronged theoretical agenda for the study of E-E. Their first agenda suggests that theoretical investigations of E-E should focus more on the variability among interventions in which researchers ought to move beyond asking merely 'what' effects E-E programs have and spend more time investigating 'how' and 'why' they have those effects. The second agenda recommends there should be greater acknowledgment of existing resistances to E-E interventions, which are identified as (a) message production, (b) message environment, and (c) message reception. Third is that E-E theorizing will benefit from close investigation of the rhetorical, play, and effective aspects. The fourth agenda for E-E recommends that 'effects' research should consider utilizing a broader understanding of individual, group, and social-level changes, giving recognition to the fact that studies to date have tended to focus on the effects of E-E interventions on the individual but have failed to consider how individuals may react differently in given situations. The fifth and final agenda proposes that E-E research should be more receptive to methodological pluralism and measurement ingenuity in which audience survey, which has been the preferred method for early E-E studies, can be complemented with other research methods such as focus group interviews, participant observation, and in-depth interviews, among others. While the recommendations of Singhal and Rogers (1999) are noteworthy, it is important to recognize that none of these recommendations should be interpreted as being intended to question the value or relevance of existing research on E-E interventions or of the value of E-E interventions themselves. Rather, they propose to help expand our understanding of the invaluable benefits to be derived from E-E.

FIRST- AND SECOND-ORDER CHANGE

To better appreciate the arguments that support the use of E-E for social change, it is essential to first understand the concept of social change. For one thing, before solving complex social problems, Watzlawick, Weakland, and Fisch (1974) advocate that social change agents must be wary about how problems are defined, as they can determine the nature of the proposed solutions especially if they are poorly defined at the individual, group, or societal levels. Consistent with the systems perspective, they further argue that change can be categorized as either 'first-order' or 'second-order'. First-order change typically examines changes in knowledge, attitudes, and practices within a given system which remain unchanged, whereas second-order change denotes a change in the system itself. Further, Singhal, Rao, and Pant (2006) describe first-order change as incremental and involving a linear progression to do more or less, better, faster, or with greater accuracy. On the other hand, second-order change calls for non-linear, lateral, and 'unconventional' approaches to solve social problems (Cooperrider & Srivastava, 1987; Kahane, 2004). Singhal et al. (2006) claim that this change essentially involves a transformation from one state to another and is facilitated by greater creativity and prolonged investment of time and contact by a change agent. They also note that when second-order change is eventually established or gains legitimacy, this state is described as 'amplification', which involves the 'spread of a second-order change from one context to another with the necessary modifications to fit the new context' (p. 274). They further argue that amplification or the spread of second-order changes occurs over a period of time and ultimately leads to a 'routinization' of 'new' values, norms, and actions in a society, creating a climate of social support and 'collective efficacy' for audience members to pursue agreed actions to achieve collective goals.

In practice, however, it is not unusual to find E-E efforts attaining both first-order and second-order changes simultaneously. Notwithstanding, it is imperative that change agents or E-E practitioners first determine which of the changes they seek in order to render these initiatives worthwhile. Although the practice of using entertainment in education has been around for some time, it has only recently developed into an area of significant academic inquiry. This is a reflection perhaps of the value academicians now place on the role that entertainment and entertainment media play in imparting formal and informal knowledge. In particular, it is recognized that although learning is a human process, many of the teaching methods currently in use fail to consider the human aspect of learning. Rather, learning has so far been measured by one's ability to memorize information in which data are inputted into students and if the data do not stick, they are inputted again. Some authorities have mixed feelings about the efficacy of this approach and question whether it truly enables effective learning to take place. In other words, whereas the approach may facilitate training through memorization, this is very different from learning because memorization takes some human elements out of the process (GED Academy, 2008).

Few would argue that learning requires one to show real progress toward a clearly defined set of goals in which progress could be measured objectively. That, however, implies more than merely reducing teaching to only a statement of skills and facts to be 'picked up' through a repetitive practice of those skills or reiteration of the facts. As learning is something that occurs inside students' minds, it is felt that students' minds must be engaged because engagement leads to motivation and motivation is the key to learning (GED Academy, 2008). It is here that entertainment becomes relevant because its very nature makes it geared toward engagement. In this regard, Murphy (1989) illustrates the value of E-E noting that when young children watch *Sesame Street,* they are not watching to learn the alphabet or because someone tells them they must. They watch *Sesame Street* because it is engaging and entertaining and includes not merely a recitation of letters and numbers or instructions in different skills but is an environment of colors, shapes, creatures, and human interactions (Murphy, 1989). Further, *Sesame Street* is a microcosm of the world and is intensified vibrantly to appeal to young viewers. As a result, young learners become engaged because engagement is a key to teaching.

With regard to E-E and its potential for social change, Singhal et al. (2006) explored how *Taru,* an entertainment-education radio soap opera, motivated individuals and communities in India's Bihar state to create their own processes of second-order change by attempting to change the system or the community. This is in contrast to the earlier focus of E-E research that was primarily engaged with first-order change examining knowledge-attitude-practice (KAP) as outcome variables (Singhal & Rogers, 1999). Notwithstanding, Singhal et al. (2006) concluded that their study calls for overcoming 'occupational psychoses' and 'trained incapacities' in conceiving and implementing social change interventions. 'Trained incapacities' and 'occupational psychoses' are states of people losing their capacity to think beyond what they are trained in, according to the thinking of philosopher Kenneth Duva Burke. Singhal et al. (2006) lament that for some time communication and social change have been preoccupied with bringing about incremental first-order change. Instead, they advocate 'a different orientation, a different world-view, and a different way to frame social problems to expand the space for solutions' (p. 282).

Similarly, television productions, along with films, museum exhibits, and computer software that uses entertainment to attract and maintain audiences, with the specific aim of incorporating educational content or messages, all represent modern forms of edutainment. Nonetheless, it has been suggested that edutainment has existed throughout human existence in the form of parables and fables. Entertainment is not only effective for young children, as in the case of *Sesame Street.* The GED Academy at Florida State College notes that as learning progresses, the drive to engage progresses as well. In this way, students should have developed self-motivation, and self-engagement at higher learning levels. Some do, but many do not. In fact, many students become disengaged as they move forward in school, and learning becomes simultaneously harder and less interesting. What the GED Academy suggests is that at every level, learning should attempt to engage the mind on a human level and in the way that humans understand the world. It is thought that literature, drama, video games, television, and films are already exploring and analyzing engagement for its own sake.

More particularly, 'if education can draw on the tools of entertainment, without losing sight of its educational goals and progress, it can become highly effective' (GED Academy, 2008).

ENTERTAINMENT-EDUCATION IN PRACTICE

On the basis of evidence to date, it is well established that E-E has had a significant impact in communicating important messages on a wide variety of topics to audiences across the globe. Examples of this can be readily found in the United States, United Kingdom, and Latin America, which have all used the technique successfully, particularly in addressing health and social issues. Some of the popular topics that have been the subject of E-E include substance abuse, immunization, teenage pregnancy, HIV/AIDS, and cancer. These topics, among others, have found attentive audiences in Latin America, where television producer Miguel Sabido has skillfully used his understanding of communication theory to produce education messages that are disseminated through the Latin *telenovela*. Miguel Sabido is a drama writer-producer for Televisia, Mexico, and is considered the father of E-E. This highly successful approach of utilizing televovelas has been credited in Latin America with raising awareness and changing behavior toward family planning and literacy.

On its official website, the Center for Disease Control and Prevention (CDC) acknowledges its recognition of the power commanded by popular entertainment in shaping viewers' perceptions and practices. In particular, the CDC (2000) notes that 'television shows, movies, and music not only command the attention of their audiences, but also reinforce existing behavior, demonstrate new behavior, and affect audience emotions' (CDC, 2000). For this reason, the CDC admits to partnering with Hollywood executives and academic, public health, and advocacy organizations to share information with writers and producers about the nation's pressing health issues. To this end, it has an established Entertainment Education Program, which provides expert consultation and education, as well as resources for writers and producers who develop scripts with health storylines, as part of a collaborative initiative with Hollywood, Health & Society (HH&S) at the Norman Lear Center of the University of Southern California (USC). The CDC (2000) recognizes popular entertainment as an ideal outlet for sharing health information and affecting behavior. Consistent with this view it is interested in providing information that covers a variety of topics including violence against women, suicide, lead poisoning, hospital infection, bioterrorism, youth health issues, HIV/AIDS and much more. Knowing that 88 percent of people in America learn about health issues from television, CDC believes that prime time and daytime television programs, movies, talk shows and more, are great outlets for its health messages.

The CDC's belief in the value of E-E is manifested in its partnership with staff of USC on research efforts designed to measure the impact of TV shows and other entertainment formats on audiences. Its basis is that 'national surveys have already shown that daytime and prime time viewers pay attention to the health information in TV shows, learn from it, act on it, and share the information with others'. Research projects have included analysis of national survey data to interpret, for example, the impact of Spanish-language media on Hispanic audiences, monitoring 30-plus TV shows that are popular among Hispanic, African American, and general audiences for health content, and assessing the impact of a prime-time TV storyline on syphilis. Such collaborations are not unique to the CDC and USC. Rather, it is now commonplace for special interest groups, which want to communicate specialized messages, to work with Hollywood-based advocacy organizations that serve as liaisons to the entertainment community via industry forums, roundtable briefings, and technical script consultations. A good example is the Designated Driver Campaign that was developed by the Center for Health Communication of the Harvard School of Public Health, which is credited as the first successful partnership with Hollywood to promote health messages in prime-time television. Over 4 years, between 1988 and 1992, more than 160 prime-time shows featured references to the campaign theme. Some included subplots, scenes, and dialogue, whereas others devoted half-hour or hour-long episodes to the subject. By 1990, almost all young adults (18–24) in the United States were familiar with, and held a favorable view of, the designated driver concept.

Not all E-E interventions, however, owe their existence to special interest groups. Some producers and scriptwriters who have interests or personal connections to particular issues may generate relevant messages themselves. Almost two decades before the Designated Driver Campaign started, an episode of the 1970s series *Happy Days* featured its central character going to the library to meet girls but leaving with a library card instead. The episode reportedly encouraged thousands of young people to take out library cards, and there was a 500% nationwide increase in demand. Whatever their sources, there is little doubt that E-E interventions have enjoyed measurable success and have carved a place for themselves in mainstream media.

Today's state-of-the-art technology, in particular computer animation technology, has introduced a whole new dimension to E-E in which specialized messages no longer rely upon entertainment products for their transmission but in which these specialized messages are themselves the entertainment products. This can be credited to the sophistication of present-day video production and video editing techniques to the extent that E-E is being redefined to mean more than simply attaching messages to established programs. An arguable case can be made out that educational content can now be packaged in a manner that would attract viewers and hold their attention entirely on its own strength.

Like the CDC and USC, the National Geographic Channel has taken a lead in developing programs that bring to life educational subjects which otherwise would be confined to the classroom. Its *Naked Science* series uses advanced television production techniques to broadcast educational content about the universe that is appealing to viewers as much for its entertainment value as for its capacity to inform them. In this way, viewers are treated to a diet of formal educational content that helps them understand the universe in which they live and be entertained simultaneously. Similar programs have been developed by television companies such as the History Channel and many others whose E-E content touches on almost every conceivable topic of academic, social, and historical interest. One might even go so far to suggest that E-E has managed to find a place for itself within the formal education sector. The concept of 'smart classes' may expand the way we think about E-E to include using visual aids, such as graphics and motion pictures displayed via projectors, to help with classroom illustrations of theoretically ambiguous concepts. These have already proved useful in helping students understand complex ideas with assistance from visual depictions. It is important to emphasize, however, that such apparatus are to be regarded as helpful tools which have potential to assist in the delivery of formal education but which were never designed to replace trained educators.

E-E is equally manifested in the cultural expressions of the twin-island Republic of Trinidad and Tobago in the form of *Ramdilla* or the dialect version of *Ramleela,* the re-enactment of the epic Ramayana celebrating the victory of Lord Rama over the tyrant King Ravana. It is significant to note that on November 25, 2005, UNESCO designated *Ramleela* as one of the 43 new masterpieces of the 'Oral and Intangible Heritages of Humanity' in need of preservation. The *Ramdilla* initiative was pioneered by Ravindra Nath Maharaj, locally called 'Raviji', and his organization, the Hindu Prachar Kendra. Essentially, this 10-day re-enactment takes place annually (September or October) in a consecrated space called the Ramleela/Ramdilla Grong (ground) located temporarily on community grounds. The story revolves around Raama, the king-designate who, due to palace intrigue, was exiled and joined by his queen-designate, Sita, and brother, Lakshman. For the indentured people of Trinidad, 'this was like their own "exile" far away from India', according to Raviji. The current version of *Baal Ramdilla* is Ramleela directed and performed mainly by children. Raviji claims that the objective is for children to see, through Ramleela, how valuable they are as community- and nation-builders. More importantly, he maintains that the young will be able to imbibe the universal lessons of the epic story and learn to apply them in everyday life. Indeed, these goals at the individual and community levels are consistent with the expectations of both first- and second order changes that result from E-E initiatives.

The Hindu Prachar Kendra can also be credited for its E-E initiative in the form of *pichakaaree* or the local Phagwa or Holi song competition in Trinidad and Tobago. While *pichakaaree* is an instrument traditionally used during Phagwa or Holi to draw up *abeer* or the liquid through a nozzle and squirt others, in Trinidad *pichakaaree* is a forum for self-expression in the form of a song. Since its inception in 1991, it has worked on the basis of a theme inspired by the relevant social issues of the day. According to Beepath (2001), there are different categories, such as social commentary and festive songs, in which participants can take part. Although *pichakaaree* holds on to traditions of Phagwa, it also succeeds in creating modifications in order to incite the participation of youths in their culture. Another dimension is the introduction of games designed especially to facilitate the participation of children. It is, therefore, evident that the novelty of *pichakaaree* is yet another example of both first- and second-order change afforded through E-E.

CONCLUSION

What these applications demonstrate clearly is the diverse means by which entertainment- education may be pursued. They lend support to the position adopted by the GED Academy at Florida State College that educating must involve much more than memorization through repetition and reiteration of facts, but that it must be engaging and needs to be delivered in a way that takes account of learners' understanding of the human world. The mere fact that so many methods of delivery are currently being pursued, combined with the real likelihood that even more innovative methods may be developed along the way, opens the door to almost endless possibilities for further research into this still emerging concept of E-E. As technologies develop further and as education themes find their way into more sophisticated entertainment productions, one of the challenges ahead will be in determining just where entertainment stops and where education begins. However, the more critical concern for E-E is its potential for social change whether it results in first- or second-order change through innovative means such as radio and television programs in India and Mexico and folk theater as obtains in Trinidad and Tobago. The possibilities for E-E are therefore numerous for enhancing development initiatives in both the developed and particularly developing nations.

REFERENCES

Beepath, R. (2001). *The history of the Hindu Prachar Kendra and its contributions to society.* Unpublished Caribbean Studies thesis, University of the West Indies, St. Augustine, Trinidad and Tobago.

Centers for Disease Control and Prevention. (2000). *Setting a research agenda for entertainment-education.* Retrieved December 11, 2011, from http://www.learcenter.org/pdf/EEReport.pdf

Cooperrider, D. L., & Srivastava, S. (1978). Appreciative enquiry in organizational life. In W. A. Pasmore & R. W. Woodman (Eds.), *Research in organizational change and development* (Vol. 1, pp. 129–169). Greenwich, CT: JAI Press.

Diaz-Bordenave, J. (1976). Communication of agricultural innovations in Latin America. In E. M. Rogers (Ed.). *Communication and Development: Critical Perspectives*, (pp. 43–62). Beverly Hills: Sage Publications.

GED Academy. (2008, December 5). *Entertainment in education: What is missing when we strip out everything but the necessities?* (Version 3). Knol. Retrieved June 4, 2010, from http://knol.google.com/k/the-ged-academy/entertainment-in-education/c0777sp7lu3i/2

Freire, P. (1971). *Education for critical consciousness*. New York: Continuum.

Kahane, A. (2004). *Solving tough problems*. San Francisco: Berrett-Koehler.

Katz, E., & Foulkes, D. (1962). On the use of mass media as escape: Clarification of a concept. *Public Opinion Quarterly, 26*, 377–388.

Murphy, R. T. (1989). *Educational effectiveness of Sesame Street: A review of the first twenty years of research, 1969–1989*. Princeton, NJ: Educational Testing Services.

Rogers, E. M. (1995). *Diffusion of innovations* (4th). New York: Free Press.

Singhal, A., & Rogers, E. M. (1999). *Entertainment-education: A communication strategy for social change*. Mahwah, NJ: Erlbaum.

Singhal, A., & Rogers, E. M. (2002). A theoretical agenda for entertainment-education. *Communication Theory, 14*(2), 117–135.

Singhal, A., Rao, N., & Pant, S. (2006). Entertainment-education and possibilities for second-order change. *Journal of Creative Communications, 1*(3), 267–283.

Sooknanan, P. (2006). Attitudes and perceptual factors in the adoption of computers in a school system: A case study of Trinidad and Tobago. *Journal of Creative Communications, 1*(3), 235–251.

Sooknanan, P. (2009). *Perceptions and attitudes in diffusion of innovations: Teachers' role in the implementation of computers in Trinidad and Tobago*. Saarbruken, Germany: VDM Verlag.

Sutton-Smith, B. (1988). Introduction to the transaction edition. In W. Stephenson (Ed.), *The play theory of mass communication* (pp. ix–xix). New Brunswick, NJ: Transaction Books.

Thomas, P. (1994). Participatory development communications: Philosophical premises. In S. A. White, K. S. Nair & J. Ashcroft (Eds.), *Participatory Communication*.

Watzlawick, P., Weakland, J., & Fisch, R. (1974). *Change: Principles of problem formation and problem re-solution*. New York: Norton.

Wolf, M. (1999). *The entertainment economy*. New York: Random House.

Wiki Dictionary. (2005). *Edutainment*. Retrieved July 6, 2010, from http://en.wikipedia.org/wiki/Entertainment-Education

Zillman, D., & Vorderer, P. (Eds.). (2000). *Media entertainment: The psychology of its appeal*. Mahwah, NJ: Erlbaum.

7 Individual Acceptance of SMS-Based E-Government Services
A Conceptual Model

Robert Goodwin and Tony Susanto

INTRODUCTION

Delivering public services through SMS (SMS-based e-government services) is becoming popular in developed and developing countries. SMS-based e-government has also been shown to enhance good governance. However, user acceptance is still an issue, as citizens' acceptance and use of the services cannot be measured by the popularity of SMS messaging and awareness of the services. This chapter reports on a study investigating the factors that influence an individual to use SMS-based e-government services. To develop a conceptual model of individual acceptance of the services, a survey of citizens' motivations to use SMS-based e-government services was conducted combined with a cross-disciplinary analysis on user acceptance of SMS and e-government services suggested by four research directions (diffusion research, adoption research, uses and gratifications, and domestication). A decomposition approach is used to formulate the constructs. The research approach and the conceptual model contribute to the literature particularly on technology adoption and e-government research. The proposed model highlights for government and e-government practitioners the potential drivers of the acceptance of SMS-based e-government services, which might help them to proactively design interventions for the services such as altering the system, advertising campaign, or training.

OVERVIEW AND BACKGROUND

Delivering public services through the SMS channel (*SMS-based e-government*) is becoming popular in developed and developing countries (*SMSe-Gov.info*, 2010). The implementation of SMS-based e-government has also been shown to enhance good governance. Experience in the Philippines, Tartu, and Mexico City showed that SMS-based e-government significantly reduced time and cost for public services; introduced a cheaper, easier, and faster information-accessing channel; improved transparency, accountability, communication, and the relationship between government and citizens; made the services and procedures easier for citizens to use; improved the district political image; increased citizen participation; and promoted e-Democracy (Bremer & Prado, 2006; Lallana, 2004; Rannu & Semevsky, 2005). Currently, the roles of SMS-based e-government are becoming more important.

Despite the popularity and the important roles of SMS-based e-government, some cases have shown that there are issues with service acceptance. Lallana (2004) and Alampay (2003) revealed that even although SMS is very popular in the Philippines, some SMS-based e-government services did not have many users. Other experiences in Denmark and Sweden also suggested that there are likely to be determinants other than the popularity of SMS and awareness of the services which influence citizens to use SMS-based e-government services (Westlund, 2008). The success stories of SMS-based e-government, the high penetration of SMS, and the advantages of the SMS technology (easy to use, low in cost, extensive in infrastructure, and available to reach the SMS users anytime, anywhere, even in areas with no Internet access) make governments assume that citizens will accept and use SMS-based services (Susanto, Goodwin, & Calder, 2008). In fact, the popularity of SMS and awareness of the benefits of SMS-based e-government do not guarantee the acceptance of SMS-based e-government services. Governments cannot justify the investment in SMS-based e-government and will not obtain the potential benefits of SMS-based e-government unless citizens actually use the services. Hence a study about what factors influence individuals to use SMS-based e-government services is necessary in order to design and deliver acceptable SMS-based e-government services.

This chapter is a part of a study on individual acceptance of SMS-based e-government services. It particularly presents a research approach leading to a conceptual model of the acceptance of SMS-based e-government services. The research approach and the conceptual model contribute to the literature on e-government and technology adoption, specifically to SMS-based e-government literature.

The rest of this chapter presents a methodology in formulating the acceptance model, presents the proposed model and details of the constructs, and provides conclusions.

RESEARCH APPROACH

To investigate the factors that influence individuals to accept SMS-based e-government services, the study conducted research using deductive and inductive approaches. Whereas in the deductive approach the factors are generated theoretically from the literature, the inductive approach generates the factors based on the empirical qualitative data of a sample. The study includes a mix of theoretical, conceptual, and empirical studies as Patel and Jacobson (2008) recommend for studies on citizen's adoption of e-government. The research approach is described in Figure 7.1 and explained below.

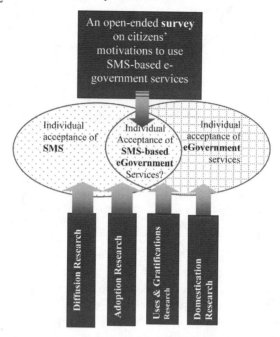

Figure 7.1   The approach of this study.

In the deductive approach, the study assumes that the determinants of individual acceptance of SMS-based e-government services may be constructed from the determinants of individual acceptance of using SMS and the determinants of using e-government services. In order to have a rich understanding of the acceptance factors, the review investigates the determinants of user acceptance of SMS and e-government services found in adoption research, diffusion research, uses and gratifications research, and domestication research (Nysveen, Pedersen, & Thorbjornsen, 2005; Pedersen & Ling, 2003). *Adoption research*, which is a mainstream research approach in information systems, could explain and predict acceptance by an individual of SMS and e-government services from psychological aspects of the user. Adoption research suggests that a new technology or service will be accepted by a group of people (target users) if each individual as a member of the group has positive beliefs toward using the service and the situations for supporting the usage are present for each individual. *Diffusion research* could explain the user acceptance of SMS and e-government services from the attributes of the technology or service and the characteristics of the adopters, with aggregates of individual users (user segments or communities) as the level of analysis. This research mainly refers to sociology, marketing, and communication disciplines (Rogers, 2003). *Uses and gratifications research*, which has its foundation in communication research, could explain what particular gratifications are sought by

Table 7.1 Individual Acceptance of e-government Services and SMS in Diffusion Research, Adoption Research, Uses and Gratifications Research, and Domestication Research

Research Directions	eGovernment Services		SMS	
	Researcher, Context, & Methodology	Core Determinants	Researcher, Context, & Methodology	Core Determinants
Diffusion research	Carter and Belanger (2004), Individual acceptance of e-government service, referring to DOI/PCI	▪ Compatibility ▪ Images ▪ Relative advantage	Mallat (2007), individual acceptance of mobile-payment, qualitative study referring to DOI	Mallat (2007), individual acceptance of mobile-payment, qualitative study
	Phang and Kankanhalli (in Titah and Barki 2005), a research framework for citizen participation via e-consultation, referring to participation theories.	▪ Incentives-related factors ▪ Resource-related factors ▪ Political institution factors ▪ Social capital factors ▪ IT factors ▪ Participation		Mallat (2007), individual acceptance of mobile-payment, ▪ qualitative study codes, service numbers, registration procedures, separate accounts burdensome) ▪ Network externalities (lack of wide merchant adoption, proprietary services/devices) ▪ Costs (premium pricing, high transaction costs) ▪ Perceived risks (unauthorized use, transaction errors, lack of transaction record and documentation, vague transactions, device and network reliability, privacy) ▪ Trust (product, service provider, telecom operators, financial institution)

Continued

Table 7.1 Continued

Research Directions	eGovernment Services		SMS	
	Researcher, Context, & Methodology	Core Determinants	Researcher, Context, & Methodology	Core Determinants
Diffusion research	Dimitrova and Chen (2006), profiling the adopters of e-government information and services, online survey.	Demographic factors relate to adoption: • Income • Age (negatively related) Psychological factors relate to adoption: • Perceived usefulness • Perceived risk tolerance (for transactional use) • Attitude Information channels • Mass media channels are more influential than interpersonal especially at early stage	Scharl et al. (2005)	• Message attributes: content; personalization; consumer control, permission and privacy. • Media attributes: Device technology, Transmission process, Product fit, Media cost.
Adoption research	Al-adawi, Yousafzai et al. (2005), individual acceptance of e-government, referring to TAM.	• Trust • Perceived risk • Perceived usefulness • Perceived ease of use	Gong and Yan (2004), Individual acceptance of SMS (as one of mobile data communication services), referring TAM, TPB, and Social Cognitive Theory.	• Intention to Use numbers, registration procedures, separate accounts burdensome) • Perceived Enjoyment • Perceived Usefulness • Perceived Ease of use • Social Norms • Self-Efficacy

Study	Factors	Study	Factors
Philip F Musa (2006), individual acceptance of general ICT for developing countries, referring to TAM and PUR.	▪ Perceived Resources ▪ Accessibility of technology to individual ▪ Individual perception of socio-economic environment ▪ Perceived Usefulness ▪ Perceived Ease of Use	Gong and Yan (2004),Individual acceptance of SMS (as one of mobile data communication services), referring TAM, TPB, and Social Cognitive Theory.	→ Domain Specific → Knowledge
		Bauer et al (in Bamba and Barnes 2006), individual acceptance of mobile-marketing	▪ Consumers' attitude toward advertising ▪ Perceived utility (perceived usefulness) ▪ Perceived risk (such as privacy and security issues) ▪ Social norms ▪ Consumers existing Knowledge
Carter and Belanger (2005 Individual acceptance of e-government service: Department of Motor Vehicle (DMV) & Department of Taxation (TAX)- Virginia) Referring to trustworthiness in e-commerce, TAM, and PCI.	▪ Compatibility ▪ Perceived Ease of Use ▪ Perceived Trustworthiness in the government agency and the technology	Wu and Wang al (in Bamba and Barnes 2006), Individual acceptance of mobile-commerce.	▪ Compatibility ▪ Ease of use ▪ Cost ▪ Perceived risk ▪ Perceive usefulness
Hung et al. (2006), public's acceptance of the online tax filing and payment system, referring to DTPB.	▪ Perceived usefulness ▪ Ease of use ▪ Perceived risk ▪ Trust ▪ Compatibility ▪ External influence	Ramayah et al. (2006) Individuals' acceptance of SMS among university students	▪ Perceived Usefulness ▪ Perceived Ease of Use

Continued

Table 7.1   Continued

Research Directions	eGovernment Services		SMS	
	Researcher, Context, & Methodology	Core Determinants	Researcher, Context, & Methodology	Core Determinants
Adoption research	Horst et. al. (2007), Dutch government, to identify the role of risk perception and trust in the intention to adopt government e-services.	■ Perceived usefulness (influenced by trust and subjective norm) ■ Perceived Risk (Weighing its benefits and risks) ■ Trust (trust on the government and involved organizations, and trust the infrastructure) ■ Perceived behavioural control	Turel et al. (2006), individuals' acceptance of SMS, referring to customer behaviour concept in marketing and technology acceptance models.	■ Behavioural intention to use SMS ■ Perceived Value: Performance/quality value, Emotional value, value for money, and social value
	Awadhi and Morris (2008), individual's acceptance of e-government services in developing country (moderators: Gender, Academic course, and Internet experience); referring to UTAUT.	■ Performance Expectancy ■ Effort Expectancy ■ Facilitating Conditions ■ Peer Influence	Wang et al. (2006), Individuals' acceptance of mobile services, Referring to TAM, TPB and Luarn & Lin's 2005 mobile banking acceptance model.	■ Behavioural intention to use SMS ■ Perceived Value: Performance/quality value, Emotional value, value for money, and social value ■ Self-efficacy ■ Perceived financial resource ■ Perceived usefulness ■ Perceived ease of use ■ Perceived credibility
	Dimitrova and Chen (2006), the effect of socio-psychological factors on adoption of e-government in US.	■ Perceived usefulness ■ Perceived uncertainty ■ Prior interest in government		

Gilbert et al. (in Titah and Barki 2005), individual' acceptance of online public service delivery. Referring to TAM, IDT, and service quality literature	• Trust and financial security • Perceived usefulness (time and cost) • Information quality	Nysveen et al. (2005), to explain intention to use SMS by integrating adoption research, uses and gratification research, and domestication research	• Motivational influences: perceived usefulness, perceived ease of use, perceived enjoyment, perceived expressiveness • Attitudinal influences (it is influenced by perceived enjoyment, usefulness, and ease of use) • Social norms • Perceived control
Lee et al. (2005), individual' acceptance of e-government, referring to TAM and trust literature.	• Trusting beliefs in e-government • Perceived Usefulness • Perceived risk	Dennis et al. (2003), individuals' adoption of SMS as a collaboration technology, referring to TAM with constructs from collaboration technology research (social presence theory, media richness theory, and the task closure model)	• Attitude toward using the technology • Perceived usefulness • Perceived ease of use • Technology characteristics (immediacy, social presence) • Individual characteristics(self-efficacy and typing speed) • Task characteristics
Treiblmaier et al. (2005), individual's acceptance of electronic payment systems, referring to TPB.	• Attitude toward e-payment • Experience • Trust in e-payment security (Influenced by experience)		
Wangpipatwong et al. (2008), citizens' continuance intention to use e-government websites, referring TAM and Computer sel-efficacy factor	• Perceived usefulness • Perceived Ease of Use • Computer efficacy		

Continued

Table 7.1 Continued

Research Directions	eGovernment Services		SMS	
	Researcher, Context, & Methodology	Core Determinants	Researcher, Context, & Methodology	Core Determinants
Uses and Gratifications research	Kaye and Johnson (2004), uses and gratifications of Internet components for political information	▪ Guidance (looking for advice) ▪ Information seeking ▪ Entertainment (relaxation and amusement purposes) ▪ Social utility (to use in discussions with others) ▪ Convenience (convenient and easier to do than traditional sources)	Hoflich and Rossler (2003), Gratifications for using SMS.	▪ Reassurance ▪ Sociability ▪ Immediate access or availability ▪ Instrumentality ▪ Entertainment or enjoyment
			Barkhuus (2005) Gratifications of SMS for individuals' social management. Diary study and interviews.	▪ Overcoming shyness (to avoid talking in public) ▪ Enabling communication without the commitment and immediate reply ▪ Social up-keeping ▪ Conciseness of messages
			Grant and Donohoe (in Wei et al. 2009), motivations of SMS use.	▪ Convenience ▪ Entertainment ▪ Social stimulation ▪ Experimental learning ▪ Escapism ▪ Seeking purchase information
			Peter et al. (in Wei et al. 2009), motives for SMS use.	▪ Entertainment ▪ Social interaction ▪ Immediate access ▪ Time management ▪ Convenience of contacting and interacting with other anywhere anytime

	Wei et al. (2009), factors affecting people to pass SMS ads to others.	▪ Prior consent ▪ Privacy concerns ▪ Instrumental (using SMS for seeking information, registering, or purchasing) ▪ Diversion (using SMS for passing time, relax, entertain, get away from what is doing) ▪ Convenience of contacting and interacting with other anywhere anytime
	Bamba and Barness (2006), Customer' permission to receive SMS marketing.	▪ Message's relevance ▪ Consumer's control over opt-in conditions ▪ Brand's familiarity consumer has high
	Krishnamurthy (in Bamba and Barnes 2006), Customer' permission to receive SMS marketing.	▪ Message relevance (message fit and attractiveness) ▪ Monetary benefit (such as incentive) ▪ Personal information entry and modification cost ▪ Message processing cost (such as cognitive load in reading message) ▪ Privacy (such as uncertainty of information misuse)
	Baron et al. (2006), to examine the embedment of SMS in UK day-to-day life and to examine limitations of TAM and UTAUT to explain consumers' behaviors toward SMS	▪ It enables interactive communication without direct talking or face-to-face ▪ It enables users to control their interpersonal interactions: can be sent anywhere anytime from any place and ubiquity (all mobile phones have SMS facility) ▪ Low cost ▪ SMS enables private communication in public places ▪ Social norms ▪ Perceived behavioral control ▪ Emotional aspects
Domestication research	Choundrie and Dwivedi (2005), Demographic and IT factors which influence adoption of e-government.	▪ Age ▪ Gender ▪ Education level ▪ Income ▪ Broadband access

an individual from using SMS and e-government services. *Domestication research*, which refers to sociology, anthropology, and ethnology, could describe and explain how new SMS and e-government services are adopted and integrated into everyday life and its societal consequences, at both the individual and the aggregate levels of analysis. Uses and gratifications research and domestication research seem relevant to the study because SMS-based e-government services exist in the context of everyday life and use is voluntary. Table 7.1 summarizes the review.

According to the review, individual acceptance of SMS or e-government services is mainly influenced by three factors: attitude toward using the service, control beliefs, and social influences. The attitudinal beliefs cover all of the perceptions about using SMS or e-government services, such as the user perceptions that using the services would overcome shyness, keep them connected with their friends, improve their social images, be compatible with their lifestyle, or enable them to obtain monetary benefits. The control beliefs refer to the self-efficacy in using the service and availability of the resources. The social influences include the pressure of social norms toward using or not using the service and the influence of mass media and personal networks.

To confirm whether the factors for individual acceptance of SMS-based e-government services have been covered by the acceptance factors of SMS

Table 7.2   Individual Motivations to Use or not to Use SMS-based e-government Services (Susanto & Goodwin, 2010).

Attitudinal beliefs	Control beliefs	Social influences
Perceived ease of use	Self-efficacy to use SMS	Mass media
Perceived cost	Availability of the device (mobile phone) and money (phone credit)	Friends
Perceived efficiency in time and distance		Family
Perceived responsiveness		Teachers
Perceived usefulness		Experts
Perceived convenience		Public figures
Trust in the SMS technology		Government officials
Perceived relevancy, quality and reliability of the information		
Perceived reliability of the mobile network		
Perceived reliability of the system performance		
Perceived good governance		
Perceived quality of public services		
Perceived compatibility		
Perceived risk to user privacy		
Perceived risk to money		

and e-government services suggested by the deductive approach, and to determine whether there are other factors, a further study was conducted using an inductive approach. The study involved a survey containing open-ended questions about individuals' motivations for using or not using SMS-based e-government services (Susanto & Goodwin, 2010). The survey was conducted in April–June 2010 and 159 responses, from 25 countries were collected by a web-based survey, paper-based questionnaires, and phone-call interviews. The majority of the respondents were from Indonesia and India (66.7%), male, 31 to 40 years old and included respondents who have Internet access and ones who do not. The survey indicated that individual motivations to use and to not use SMS-based e-government services could be also classified under attitudinal beliefs, control beliefs, and social influences (Table 7.2).

A CONCEPTUAL MODEL OF INDIVIDUAL ACCEPTANCE OF SMS-BASED E-GOVERNMENT SERVICES

On the basis of the findings and analysis in the deductive and inductive approaches, a conceptual model of individual acceptance of SMS-based e-government services was developed (Figure 7.2). Definitions of the constructs are presented in Table 7.3.

The proposed model suggests the following:

- An individual is more likely to use an SMS-based e-government service (U) when he or she has a high intention to use the service (UI) *and* perceives he or she is able to use the service (PBC) [*Hypothesis 1*].
- An intention to use SMS-based e-government (UI) is guided by three salient beliefs: *perceived behavioral control* (PBC), *attitude toward using the service* (A), and *social influences* (SI). A person is likely to intend to use an SMS-based e-government service (UI) when he or she perceives he or she is able to use the service (PBC), has a more favorable attitude toward using the service (A), and/or there is positive social influence toward the service (SI). [*Hypotheses 2,3,4*]
- This model decomposes the salient beliefs into their dimensions specifically for the SMS-based e-government service context. By decomposing the beliefs, the proposed model provides more details of the factors involved in the adoption process for SMS-based e-government services, explains the relationships among the factors, provides a stable set of beliefs that can be applied across a variety of community settings, and enables government focus on specific beliefs that may influence the adoption and be used in systems design and implementation strategies. The decomposition of the salient beliefs of individual acceptance of SMS-based e-government services is a novel contribution of this study. This study suggests that the dimensions of *perceived*

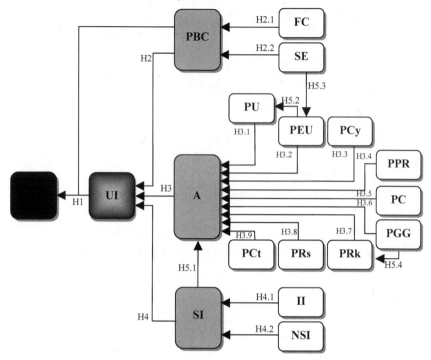

Figure 7.2   A conceptual model of individual acceptance of SMS-based e-government services.

behavioral control (PBC) consist of *facilitating conditions* (FC) and *self-efficacy* (SE); the dimensions of *attitude* toward using SMS-based e-government services include *perceived usefulness* (PU), *perceived ease of use* (PEU), *perceived compatibility* (PCy), *perceived personal relationships* (PPR), *perceived convenience* (PC), *perceived good governance* (PGG), *perceived risk* (PRk), *perceived responses* (PRs), and *perceived cost* (PCt); and the dimensions of *social influences* (SI) consist of *informational influence* (II) and *normative social influence* (NSI). [*Hypotheses 2.1–4.2*]

- Additionally, this model suggests *crossover effects* among the dimensions of the salient beliefs. First, it suggests that *social influences* (SI) has a positive relationship with *attitude* toward using the service (A); second, *perceived ease of use* (PEU) has a positive relationship with *perceived usefulness* (PU); third, *self-efficacy* to use an SMS-based e-government service (SE) has a positive relationship with *perceived ease of use of the service* (PEU); and finally *perceived good governance* (PGG) has a positive relationship with *perceived risk to use the service* (PRk). [*Hypotheses 5.1–5.4*]

Table 7.3 Definitions of the Constructs

	Construct	Definitions
U	Usage behavior	Behaviour of using an SMS-based e-government service.
UI	Usage intention to use the service	A measure of strength of one's intention to use an SMS-based e-government service (Davis, et al., 1989).
PBC	Perceived behavioural control	The extent to which a person perceives that the required opportunities and resources to use an SMS-based e-government service are available for him or her (Ajzen, 1991).
FC	Facilitating conditions	The availability of resources needed to use an SMS-based e-government service (a mobile phone or SMS device, money or phone credit, and mobile network) (Taylor & Todd, 1995).
SE	Self-efficacy	An individual's self-confidence in his/her ability to use an SMS-based e-government service (Taylor & Todd, 1995).
A	Attitude toward using the service	The degree to which individual's favourable or unfavourable evaluations toward using an SMS-based e-government service (Fishbein & Ajzen, 1975).
PU	Perceived usefulness	The degree to which a person perceives that an SMS-based e-government service is relevant to and fulfil the ones needs (Davis, et al., 1989).
PEU	Perceived ease of use	The degree to which a person perceives that an SMS-based e-government service is easy to use (Davis, et al., 1989).
PCy	Perceived compatibility	The degree to which a citizen perceives that the service is consistent with the existing public service channels and the popular communication media, and the information or service is suitable being delivered by SMS.
PPR	Perceived personal relationships	The degree to which individual perceives that using the services enables him or her to communicate directly and in-person with the decision maker.
PC	Perceived convenience	The degree to which a person perceives that the SMS-based service makes the public service easier and comfortable to access.
PGG	Perceived good governance	The degree to which a person perceives that the organization (the service provider) has implemented good governance principles.
PRk	Perceived risk	The degree to which a person believes that using the service might cause problems for him/her.

Continued

Table 7.3   Continued

	Construct	Definitions
PRs	Perceived responsiveness	The degree to which a person perceives that the service will respond any SMS sent quickly, appropriately and satisfactorily.
PCt	Perceived cost	The degree to which a person perceives that the service is costly.
SI	Social influences	The degree to which individual perceives that other people behaviors or opinions are important toward decision to use or not to use the service.
II	Informational influence	The degree to which a person perceives that the opinions or usage of the service by those who are seen as credible can be as a reference toward using the service.
NSI	Normative social influence	The degree to which a person perceives that most people think he/she should or should not use the service in question.

Related studies supporting the hypotheses are presented in Table 7.4.

As the Six Level model of SMS-based e-government (Susanto et al., 2008) suggests that there are at least six kinds of SMS-based public services, the acceptance factors are likely to be different across service categories (Bamba & Barnes, 2006; Mallat, 2007; Nysveen et al., 2005; Scharl, Dickinger, & Murphy, 2005).

Table 7.4   The Research Hypotheses and the Supporting Studies

Hypotheses		Supporting studies
I. The causes of *actual behaviour* of using SMS-based e-government services		
H1	U ← UI + PBC	(Ajzen, 1991; Davis, et al., 1989; Turel, Serenko, & Bontis, 2006; Venkatesh, Morris, Davis, & Davis, 2003)
II. The causes of intention to use SMS-based e-government services		
H2	PBC → UI	(Awadhi & Morris, 2008; Bamba & Barnes, 2006; Gong & Yan, 2004; Horst, Kuttschreuter, & Gutteling, 2007; Hung, Chang, & Yu, 2006; Susanto & Goodwin, 2010; Titah & barki, 2005)
H3	A → UI	
H4	SI → UI	

Continued

Table 7.4 Continued

III. The dimensions of attitude, social norms, and perceived behavioural control	
3.a. Perceived behavioural control beliefs	
H2.1	FC → PBC	(Al-Adawi, Yousafzai, & Pallister, 2005; Awadhi & Morris, 2008; Horst, et al., 2007; Hung, et al., 2006; Philip, 2006; Susanto & Goodwin, 2010; Taylor & Todd, 1995; Turel, et al., 2006)
H2.2	SE → PBC	(Al-Adawi, et al., 2005; Awadhi & Morris, 2008; Horst, et al., 2007; Hung, et al., 2006; Philip, 2006; Susanto & Goodwin, 2010; Taylor & Todd, 1995)
3.b. Attitudinal beliefs	
H3.1	PU → A	(Al-Adawi, et al., 2005; Awadhi & Morris, 2008; Bamba & Barnes, 2006; Gong & Yan, 2004; Hung, et al., 2006; Mallat, 2007; Philip, 2006; Scharl, Dickinger, & Murphy, 2005; Susanto & Goodwin, 2010)
H3.2	PEU → A	(Al-Adawi, et al., 2005; Awadhi & Morris, 2008; Davis, et al., 1989; Gong & Yan, 2004; Hung, et al., 2006; Mallat, 2007; Philip, 2006; Rogers, 2003; Scharl, et al., 2005; Susanto & Goodwin, 2010; Taylor & Todd, 1995; Venkatesh, et al., 2003)
H3.3	PCy → A	(Al-Adawi, et al., 2005; Awadhi & Morris, 2008; Bamba & Barnes, 2006; Davis, et al., 1989; Gong & Yan, 2004; Hung, et al., 2006; Mallat, 2007; Philip, 2006; Rogers, 2003; Scharl, et al., 2005; Susanto & Goodwin, 2010; Taylor & Todd, 1995; Venkatesh, et al., 2003)
H3.4	PPR → A	(Gong & Yan, 2004; Nysveen, et al., 2005; Turel, et al., 2006)
H3.5	PC → A	(Barkhuus, 2005; Baron, Petterson, & Haris, 2006; Gong & Yan, 2004; Nysveen, et al., 2005; Turel, et al., 2006)
H3.6	PGG → A	(Al-Adawi, et al., 2005; Awadhi & Morris, 2008; Hung, et al., 2006; Mallat, 2007; Philip, 2006; Scharl, et al., 2005; Susanto & Goodwin, 2010)

Continued

Table 7.4   Continued

Hypotheses		Supporting studies
H3.7	PRk → A	(Al-Adawi, et al., 2005; Awadhi & Morris, 2008; Bamba & Barnes, 2006; Gong & Yan, 2004; Hung, et al., 2006; Mallat, 2007; Philip, 2006; Susanto & Goodwin, 2010)
H3.8	PRs → A	(Susanto & Goodwin, 2010)
H3.9	PCt → A	(Susanto & Goodwin, 2010; Turel, et al., 2006)
3.c. Social norms		
H4.1	II → SI	(Kelman, 1958; Susanto & Goodwin, 2010)
H4.2	NSI → SI	(Awadhi & Morris, 2008; Bamba & Barnes, 2006; Barkhuus, 2005; Baron, et al., 2006; Gong & Yan, 2004; Hung, et al., 2006; Kaye & Johnson, 2004; Kelman, 1958; Rogers, 2003; Turel, et al., 2006; Wei, Xiaoming, & Pan, 2009)
Crossover effects among the dimensions		
H5.1	SI → A	(Kelman, 1958; Susanto & Goodwin, 2010)
H5.2	PEU → A	(Al-Adawi, et al., 2005; Davis, et al., 1989; Gong & Yan, 2004; Hung, et al., 2006; Mallat, 2007; Philip, 2006; Rogers, 2003; Scharl, et al., 2005; Taylor & Todd, 1995)
H5.3	SE → PEU	(Gong & Yan, 2004)
H5.4	PGG → PRk	(Susanto & Goodwin, 2010)

CONCLUSIONS AND CURRENT STUDY

This chapter reported on a study that investigated factors that influence individuals to use SMS-based e-government services. To develop a conceptual model of individual acceptance of SMS-based e-government services, the study comprehensively referred to empirical data from a survey of citizens' motivations to use SMS-based e-government services (inductive approach) combined with theories and findings on user acceptance of SMS and e-government services, diffusion research, adoption research, uses and gratification research, and domestication research (deductive approach).

The proposed model suggests that there are nine attitudinal beliefs, two control beliefs, and two dimensions of social influences related to individuals that should be addressed by government and e-government practitioners in designing and delivering SMS-based e-government services in order to minimize citizens' resistance toward using the services. Currently, the model is under empirical investigation. The model will be validated across four different services according to the Six Level model of SMS-based e-government: *Listen, Notification, Pull-based information,* and *Transaction* services.

REFERENCES

Ajzen, I. (1991). The theory of planned behavior. *Organizational Behaviour and Human Decision Processes, 50*(2), 179–211.

Al-Adawi, Z., Yousafzai, S., & Pallister, J. (2005). *Conceptual model of citizen adoption e-government.* Paper presented at the Second International Conference on Innovations in Information Technology.

Alampay, E. A. (2003). *Text 2920/117: Reporting police wrongdoing via SMS in the Philippines.* eGovernment for Development. Retrieved November 8, 2011, from http://www.egov4dev.org/mgovernment/resources/case/text2920.shtml

Awadhi, S. A., & Morris, A. (2008). *The use of the UTAUT model in the adoption of e-government services in Kuwait.* Paper presented at the Hawaii International Conference on System Sciences.

Bamba, F., & Barnes, S. J. (2006, June). *Evaluating consumer permission in SMS advertising.* Paper presented at the Fifth Mobility Roundtable, Helsinki, Finland.

Barkhuus, L. (2005). *Why everyone loves to text message: Social management with SMS.* Paper presented at the GROUP'05, Sanibel Island, FL. .

Baron, S., Petterson, A., & Haris, K. (2006). Beyond technology acceptance: Understanding consumer practice. *International Journal of Service Industry Management, 17*(2), 111–135.

Bremer, A. A., & Prado, L. A. L. (2006). *Municipal m-services using SMS.* Paper presented at the Euro mGov 2006.

Carter, L. and F. Belanger (2004). The influence of perceived characteristics of innovation on e-government adoption. *Electronic Journal of E-Government, 2*(1), 11–20.

Choudrie, J. and Y. Dwivedi (2005). *A survey of citizens' awareness and adoption of e-government initiatives, the 'government gateway': a United Kingdom perspective.* Paper presented at eGovernment Workshop Brunel University, West London, UK, Brunel University.

Dennis, A.R., Venkatesh, V., Ramesh, V. (2003). Adoption of Collaboration Technologies: Integrating Technology Acceptance and Collaboration Technologies Research. Indiana University, USA . *Sprouts: Working Papers on Information Systems, 3*(8).

Dimitrova, D. V. and Y.-C. Chen (2006). Profiling the Adopters of E-Government Information and Services. *Social Science Computer Review* 24(2), 172–188.

Davis, F. D., Bagozzi, R. P., & Warshaw, P. W. (1989). User acceptance of computer technology: A comparison of two theoretical models. *Management Science, 35*(8), 982–1003.

Fishbein, M., & Ajzen, I. (1975). *Belief, attitude, intention, and behavior: An introduction to theory and research.* Boston: Addison-Wesley.

Gong, M., & Yan, X. (2004). *Applying technology acceptance model, theory of planned behavior and social cognitive theory to mobile data communications service acceptance.* Paper presented at the Pacific Asia Conference on Information Systems (PACIS).

Horst, M., Kuttschreuter, M., & Gutteling, J. M. (2007). Perceived usefulness, personal experiences, risk perception and trust as determinants of adoption of e-government services in the Netherlands. *Computers in Human Behavior, 23*(4), 1838–1852.

Hung, S.-Y., Chang, C.-M., & Yu, T.-J. (2006). Determinants of user acceptance of the e-government services: The case of online tax filling and payment system. *Government Information Quarterly, 23*, 97–122.

Kaye, B. K., & Johnson, T. J. (2004). A Web for all reasons: Uses and gratifications of Internet components for political information. *Telematics and Informatics, 21*, 197–223.

Kelman, H. C. (1958). Compliance, identification, and internalization: Three processes of attitude change. *Journal of Conflict Resolution, 2*(1).

Lallana, E. C. (2004). *SMS, business and government in the Philippines.* Manila, the Philippines: DOST.

Lee, J. K., S. Braynov, H.R. Rao (2005). *Effects of a Public Emergency on Citizens' Usage Intention toward E-Government: A Study in the Context of War in Iraq.* Presented at the Eleventh Americas Conference on Information Systems Omaha, NE, USA.

Mallat, N. (2007). Exploring consumer adoption of mobile payments: A qualitative study. *Journal of Strategic Information Systems, 16*, 413–432.

Musa, P. F. (2006). Making a case for modifying the technology acceptance model to account for limited accessibility in developing countries. *Information Technology for Development, 12*(3), 213–224.

Nysveen, H., Pedersen, P. E., & Thorbjornsen, H. (2005). Intentions to use mobile services: Antecedents and cross-service comparisons. *Journal of the Academy of Marketing Science, 33*(3), 330–346.

Patel, H., & Jacobson, D. (2008). *Factors influencing citizen adoption of e-government: A review and critical assessment.* Paper presented at the 16th European Conference on Information Systems, Galway, Ireland.

Pedersen, P. E., & Ling, R. (2003). Modifying adoption research for mobile Internet service adoption: Cross-disciplinary interactions. In *Proceedings of the 36th Hawaii International Conference on System Sciences.* New York: IEEE.

Ramayah, T., Yulihasri, et al. (2006). Predicting Short Message Service (SMS) Usage among university students using the Technology Acceptance Model (TAM). Presented at *IAMOT,* Malaysia.

Rannu, R., & Semevsky, M. (2005). *Mobile services in Tartu.* Tartu, Estonia: Mobi Solutions.

Rogers, E. M. (2003). *Diffusion of innovations* (5th ed.). New York: Free Press.

Scharl, A., Dickinger, A., & Murphy, J. (2005). Diffusion and success factors of mobile marketing. *Electronic Commerce Research and Applications, 4*, 159–173.

Susanto, T. D., & Goodwin, R. (2010). Factors influencing citizen adoption of SMS-based e-government services. *Electronic Journal of E-Government, 8*(1), 55–70.

Susanto, T. D., Goodwin, R., & Calder, P. (2008). *A six-level model of SMS-based e-government.* Paper presented at the International Conference on E-Government 2008.

Taylor, S., & Todd, P. A. (1995). Understanding information technology usage: A test of competing models. *Information Systems Research, 6*(2), 144–176.

Titah, R., & Barki, H. (2005). e-Government Adoption and Acceptance: a Literature Review . Cahier de la Chaire de recherche du Canada en implantation et gestion des technologies de l'information, 05 (03), HEC Montreal.

Treiblmaier, H., A. Pinterits, et al. (2004). *Antecedents of the Adoption of EPayment Services in the Public Sector.* Presented at Twenty-Fifth International Conference on Information Systems.

Turel, O., Serenko, A., & Bontis, N. (2006). User acceptance of wireless short messaging services: Deconstructing perceived value. *ScienceDirect, 44*(2007), 63–73.

Venkatesh, V., Morris, M. G., Davis, G. B., & Davis, F. D. (2003). User acceptance of information technology: Toward a unified view. *MIS Quarterly, 27*(3), 425–478.

Wang, Y.-S., H.-H. Lin, P. Luarn. (2006). Predicting consumer intention to use mobile service. *Info System,* 16, 157–179.

Wangpipatwong, S., W. Chutimaskul, et al. (2008). Understanding Citizen's Continuance Intention to Use e-Government Website: a Composite View of Technology Acceptance Model and Computer Self-Efficacy. *The Electronic Journal of e-Government,* 6(1), 55–64.

Wei, R., Xiaoming, H., & Pan, J. (2009). Examining user behavioral response to SMS ads: Implications for the evolution of the mobile phone as a bona-fide medium. *Telematics and Informatics,* 27, 32–41.

Westlund, O. (2008). *Towards an understanding of the adoption and use of mobile Internet news.* preceding Roskilde Universitetscenter.

8 The Role of Institutional Entrepreneurs in Enabling the Adoption of E-Governance Systems

Anuradha Mundkur

INTRODUCTION

Not enough attention is paid to how information systems used by governments are designed, adopted, and institutionalized. Since information systems 'encapsulate the structures, routines, norms, and values implicit in the rich contexts within which they are embedded' (Benbasat & Zmud, 2003, p. 186), they are shaped by social factors (key stakeholders, conflicts, power moves, symbolic acts, etc.) and technological factors (existing technology infrastructures, technical know-how, skills). The trajectory from design to adoption to institutionalization is not pre-determined but contingent upon broad social contexts, specifically the significant role by institutional entrepreneurs. Institutional entrepreneurs can be described as e-champions—'leaders with vision who put e-governance onto the agenda and make it happen' (Heeks, 2001, p. 20). Institutional entrepreneurs may purposively or unwittingly encode structural biases into information systems (Winner, 1986), as a result of which these systems structure subsequent actions in particular ways, creating a path-dependent development trajectory. This chapter moves away from treating information systems as a black box. In doing so it unpacks how information systems become institutionalized rather than assume embeddedness.

To highlight the dynamic relationship between the design, adoption, and institutionalization of e-governance systems and the role of institutional entrepreneurs, this chapter uses the deployment of a financial management system by an Urban Local Body (ULB), the third tier of government (local government), in a southern city in India as its case.[1]

OVERVIEW AND BACKGROUND

There is little doubt that information and communication technology (ICT) enables us to disseminate large volumes of information in a timely and cost-effective manner. For many governments the technology push argument, that ICTs can be used to make them more efficient (through enabling cross-agency functioning), transparent, and accountable, led to significant investments in implementing e-governance systems. E-governance was also perceived by policymakers as an opportunity to deal with performance and confidence deficit (Nye, 2001) and to realize the goals of administrative reform movements such as New Public Management, which advocates a business-oriented approach to government (Boston, Martin, Pallot, & Walsh, 1996; Hood, 1995; Ingraham, 1997).

Over the past few years, India has registered significant improvements in e-governance rankings (Hafeez, 2004) and won awards, such as the Stockholm Challenge and Commonwealth Award, for its efforts in applying information technology to create better services for citizens. This chapter looks at one such project implemented in a city in the southern Indian state of Karnataka. This city has emerged as a global technology center, and the financial management system deployed by its ULB was part of an effort to create a SMART (Simple, Moral, Accountable, Responsive, and Transparent) government (Sachdeva, 2002).

In 2000 the ULB began reforming its financial management practices. The introduction of an e-governance system, namely a financial management system, which combined modern accounting practices with a management information system (which I will call F-MIS), was an integral part of the reform. To achieve this transformation, the ULB partnered with a task force (TF) established in 2000 by the head of state at that time. The TF comprised a voluntary group of information technology companies and eminent citizens. Its mandate was to upgrade and enhance the managerial and administrative capabilities of various civic and administrative bodies such as the ULB. Working with the ULB to streamline its financial management system was one of TF's first projects. A core project team was established comprising members from the ULB's executive, a member from the TF who took on the role of the project team leader, a consultant hired by the TF, two retired State Accounts Department officers and 20 young graduates.

The F-MIS was designed such that all types of users, from citizens to policymakers, could access information in formats that they could easily understand and interpret. Backed by a single database, F-MIS allowed all levels of management to access information in a timely manner as there were no longer any delays in compiling information from various sources. It also provided a base for reviewing and monitoring past decisions taken by the ULB's senior and executive management. ULB employees could access information regarding the status of various financial records they updated and managed reducing their workload on routine items; decision makers could access various reports needed for planning; policymakers and funding agencies could access reports to evaluate the performance of the ULB.[2] At the time of conducting this study (2005–2006), there was talk of creating a web-enabled section of the F-MIS through which citizens could access information about the revenue planning, actual collection, details on budgeted projects, and project status.

Supporting F-MIS was a citizens' movement for transparency and accountability, PROOF (Public Record of Operations and Finance). Launched by four city-based non-government organizations, PROOF used the quarterly statement of the ULB as a starting point in an exercise to track financial statements, develop performance indicators for different expenditures, and create a space for dialogue between the ULB and citizens on whether the expenditures on development projects were adding any value. Another spin-off was the 'Arthika Darpana' (Financial Mirror). Under this initiative, complete financial information about each ward[3] was given to the elected representative, including information on budget allocation, progress of development projects, and status of revenue collection. The same information was also available to the public (NIUA, 2004; Vithayathil, 2004).

THE ROLE OF INSTITUTIONAL ENTREPRENEURS

E-governance literature, both academic and anecdotal, points to the important role played by e-champions (or institutional entrepreneurs) in pushing e-governance projects like F-MIS to their logical conclusion (Narayan, Nerurkar, & Mehta, 2006). Studies have suggested that, among other factors, the loss of e-champions (or institutional entrepreneurs) often results in the failed implementation of e-governance projects. However, what these studies have failed to explore is how e-champions bring about institutional change. The work of institutional entrepreneurs is the focus of this chapter.

In this case study, the institutional entrepreneurs were the executive management of the ULB and the TF, particularly the project team leader and the consultant hired by the TF. The project team leader and the consultant acted as catalysts to enable the ULB to reform its financial management practices by providing financial resources, intellectual capital, and labor to engage in the reform process. Citizens, their organizations, and elected representatives from the wards (comprising the ULB Council), were perceived as belonging to a group of stakeholders outside the ULB. That is, they were grouped along with the state and national governments and other financial institutions to which the ULB must disclose its financial position. As a result the involvement of these stakeholders was limited to accessing financial reports generated by F-MIS. From the beginning, the project was conceptualized in two phases—first instituting internal reforms to 'clean up' information bottlenecks in the ULB through the introduction of modern financial management practices led by F-MIS, and second creating a citizen's platform that could use the information to hold the ULB accountable for its actions through public disclosure forums and participative budgeting. Elected representatives of the ULB Council were left out of both processes. Citizens and civil society organizations were excluded from phase one but were seen to play a lynchpin role in phase two.

Why is the exclusion significant? Looking at who was excluded highlights interests that are *not* inscribed in the systems design. Thus, for instance, initially F-MIS was not web-enabled, which meant that every time an elected representative or citizen or civil society organization wanted information they had to approach the Additional Commissioner of Finance. This perpetuated a dependency relationship that kept existing structural power centers in place. Although the institutional entrepreneurs saw the exclusion of elected representatives as an unintended oversight, evidence suggests their exclusion was deliberate. They feared that the project might be hijacked given the highly political nature of some appointments within the ULB. This is corroborated by the project report on F-MIS where in the section titled 'Lessons Learned', which provides a check list for transforming financial management systems in ULBs, there is a call for implementing changes as 'administrative reforms' rather than as a 'political mandate'. The exclusion of elected representatives is problematic because they play a significant role in the allocation of funds to different schemes and projects acting as links between citizens and the ULB (Benjamin & Bhuvaneswari, 2001; Ghosh, 2005; Vijayalakshmi, 2004).

INSTITUTIONAL LOGICS AND FRAMING

The wider socio-cultural and political milieu provided institutional entrepreneurs with concepts and frameworks to legitimate the push for a change in ULB's financial management practices. National policies such as the 74th constitutional amendment conceptualized local governments, like the ULB, as self-governing units. Not only would they have more control over budget allocations, their access to financial resources was no longer restricted to grants provided by state governments. Coupled with the fact that state grants to ULBs for infrastructure development projects was steadily decreasing, these bodies were forced to resort to market-based financing. However, this required ULBs to be seen as creditworthy.

This notion of creditworthiness became the institutional entrepreneurs' mantra. It is impossible to assess whether or not an organization is creditworthy unless there are modern financial management practices that enable such an analysis. Hence, it became imperative that the outdated manual financial management practice of the ULB be replaced by a more rigorous system. The introduction of F-MIS gained greater legitimacy as institutional entrepreneurs drew on recommendations made by a national level task force on accounting and budget formats for local governments, instituted by the Comptroller and Auditor General of India. Several reform-linked funding schemes such as the National Urban Renewal Mission (NURM), which imposed conditions on receiving funds for infrastructure development projects, such as modernizing financial management practices, provided compelling reasons to adopt F-MIS. Finally, laws and regulations passed at the state level also provided institutional entrepreneurs with the much needed legitimacy. The Karnataka Right to Information Act (2000) required all government institutions to maintain records of their activities in a manner such that they could be easily accessed by citizens. It also required all levels of government to publish, on a regular basis, relevant facts concerning important decisions and policies affecting the public. In order to comply with this requirement, institutional entrepreneurs argued that the ULB needed to be in a position to access critical information related to its budget, revenue, expenditures, and other financial data. The F-MIS system was designed to do precisely that.

Binding all the previously mentioned arguments together was the compelling institutional logic of good governance characterized by practices that are equitable, accountable, transparent, efficient, and participative. The principles of good governance served as institutional logics to frame the work around F-MIS. Institutional logics act as 'organizing principles that are accessible for organizations and individuals in terms of further development of micro-processes through which the meaning of what has happened, what is happening, and what is going to happen is constructed' (Hwang & Powell, 2006, p. 196). Drawing on existing notions of good governance as articulated by organizations such as the World Bank and Asian Development Bank, institutional entrepreneurs believed that good governance could be achieved through effective management, whose dimensions included public sector management, accountability, a legal framework for development, information, and transparency (Asian Development Bank, 1995). Finance-related information was made central to each of these dimensions. Thus, accountability 'is facilitated by evaluation of their economic and financial performance . . . and efficiency in resource use' (Asian Development Bank, 1995, p. 9). Participation implied that government structures are flexible so that they can provide citizens the opportunity to improve the design and implementation of public programs by voicing their priorities in budget allocations. Transparency was linked to the availability of information 'especially relevant in the case of those sectors that are intrinsically information intensive, such as the financial sector' (Asian Development Bank, 1995, p. 12).

The problem facing the ULB was defined as the lack of information needed for good decision making. Good decision making, which lies at the heart of good governance, is characterized by accountable, transparent, and participative decision-making processes. Since most of government decision making concerns the efficient allocation and monitoring of resources, institutional entrepreneurs argued that what the ULB lacked was a system providing timely and accurate financial data on which to base decisions. In turn, this lack of financial information made it difficult for citizens to evaluate the performance of the ULB resulting in a lack of accountability and transparency. Where the TF and the ULB differed was on what good decision making meant. For the TF an integral aspect of good decision making was the participation of citizens in the process, but for the ULB good decision making implied the ability to respond in a quick and efficient manner to demands for changes in resource allocation. So while the TF emphasized that in order to consistently make good decisions there is a need for good quality information as well as a rigorous and transparent process by which decisions were made, for the ULB the emphasis was on the former.

It was logical therefore to focus on the Finance Department, as it was the repository of the information needed to make good decisions. This focus on financial management was in keeping with ideas put forth by international organizations such as the Asian Development Bank that identified public expenditure management as instrumental to achieving sound development and being the core business of governments. *The solution presented itself from the way in which the problem was framed.* If the ULB needed access to timely and accurate financial data for decision making, then two things needed to happen. First, the introduction of modern financial management practices so that the ULB would be in a position to assess its revenues, expenditures, assets, and liabilities and make policy decisions based on them rather than the current guesswork. Second, a process had to be put in place so that the information could be accessed and analyzed on demand; in other words, commission an F-MIS.

Institutional entrepreneurs used different vocabularies to ensure that the manner in which the issue was framed resonated with different people. Thus, for example, when talking with middle management, emphasis was laid on being able to supervise the work of the lower level staff; for senior management, the benefit involved better planning and management; and for the lower level staff, it was about reducing the workload. By constructing cultural frames, 'which are representations of collective problems and solutions that help other actors to link their own interests and identities to a collective purpose' (Stone-Sweet, Fligstein, & Sandholtz, 2001, p. 1), they shaped the terms and conditions within which the project takes place.

Institutional entrepreneurs are not 'disinterested altruistic agents of greater systemic effectiveness or efficiency. To the contrary, their advocacy is impossible to separate from their own particular material and ideal interests . . . Though they rely on myths and institutional formulas to articulate and legitimate their proposals for structural change, they do so in innovative ways while simultaneously challenging and critiquing existing arrangements, rules of thought and standardized practices' (Colomy, 1998, p. 271). They use their professional knowledge to redefine what practices and structures are appropriate (Hwang & Powell, 2006). This is very well illustrated by the present case. In the case of the F-MIS project, the institutional entrepreneurs had a similar background. They were bankers, chartered accountants, and individuals familiar with financial management standards followed by commercial enterprises. By 'transposing institutional logics from one domain where they are common and accepted into a new, unfamiliar domain' (Hwang & Powell, 2006, p. 199), they facilitate the adoption of new practices. F-MIS and its financial reporting standards are nothing new in the world of commercial enterprises. Since there was a high level of uncertainty regarding how one should proceed with reforming the financial management systems in local government, the institutional entrepreneurs were able to use their professional knowledge and expertise to provide a methodology that could be followed. The argument, as the project team leader put was, 'when companies that operate in 106 countries with 99 currencies and multiple businesses could present their performance statement to the world, why couldn't the ULB, which has an operating radius of about 8 km and which deals in a single currency?,' (Prayag, 2004). By using their professional knowledge and expertise the institutional entrepreneurs, in this case, acted as filtering agents, interpreting laws and regulations (the constitutional amendment, and the technical guide to accounting and budget reforms for local government) and formulating appropriate strategies to ensure compliance.

Institutional entrepreneurs openly called for changes in the existing financial management system. Several channels were used to get their message out—the mainstream print media (articles written by the TF, particularly the project team leader and the consultant); journals and newsletters published by the four non-government organizations involved in PROOF; and seminars and public forums, organized by local and international organizations. White papers written by the TF and the core project team were shared with leading policymakers at the state and national levels. The common theme running through all these publications was the need to reform financial management practices to ensure good governance and the propagation of F-MIS as a means to achieve this goal. The induction of these institutional entrepreneurs as members of national level committees on local government reform, such as the National Urban Renewal Mission, only served to give the project greater legitimacy.

Projects like F-MIS require a range of skill sets to enable their successful deployment. Hwang and Powell (2006) point out that institutional entrepreneurs act as connectors bringing together groups that would otherwise not interact. In the F-MIS project this is best exemplified by the project team leader. He was able to bring in the consultant and his team to work on the implementation of the project; a local chartered accountant was roped in to provide article clerks who did the entire mapping of the business process; and local software company, where the project team leader was an investor, offered to build the necessary software free of cost. Equally significant is the fact that the project was able to secure funding for the entire project from a trust run by the chair of the TF. The project team leader was also able to use his social circle and collaboration with other civil society organizations to launch PROOF. The launching of PROOF was an important component to ensure the institutionalization of F-MIS. It provided the demand side of the equation. By creating a platform where citizens could access, analyze, and debate financial statements disseminated by the ULB, PROOF ensured that there would always be steady demands for the reports generated by F-MIS. It was also the TF's way of realizing its primary motivation behind engaging with the ULB—enabling participatory governance.

INSTITUTIONALIZATION AND PATH CREATION

Following Frumkin and Kaplan (2000), the process of institutionalization can be seen as one that begins with a trigger that breaks 'previously recurrent actions and reflexive behaviour of individuals' (p. 8). These triggers can be economic or political, or, as in the F-MIS case, 'a radical transformation in the intellectual lenses through which people look at and understand their world' (p. 9). The new notions of good governance challenged the existing arrangements of governmental decision making by putting forth a model that emphasized transparency, accountability, and citizens' participation in decision making. Institutional entrepreneurs responded to these changes by 'by bringing it to the attention of others and by proposing a response that carries weight' (p. 12). These entrepreneurs, through framing, advocacy, and persuasion attempt to change the beliefs and practices of other actors (Benford, & Snow, 2000). If they succeed, then new beliefs and practices become embedded in the day-to-day routines of the organization and diffuse to other organizations as well.

An important dimension of the work institutional entrepreneurs engage in can be described as *path creation*. The term suggests that institutional entrepreneurs behave in a proactive manner to 'make sense, enact and shape events and opportunities, often in ways other than those prescribed the existing rules and norms' (Grand & MacLean, 2003, p. 7). Thus, rather than passive observers reacting to events, institutional entrepreneurs 'attempt to shape paths, in specific contexts and in real time, by setting processes in motion that actively shape emerging practices, artefacts and procedures' (p. 7). The act of framing itself can be seen as an attempt at path creation. By setting the agenda early on, institutional entrepreneurs 'set where the groups are going and what their collective identity is likely to be' (Fligstein, 1997, p. 399). Linking the poor quality of decision making to poor quality information, the institutional entrepreneurs were able to focus their efforts on enabling the existing decision-making processes rather than move for a radical change to the institutional environment which dictates how decisions are made. However, while framing initiates the creation of a path, by itself it is insufficient to sustain and institutionalize the path.

According to Colomy (1998), 'few challenge every recognizable feature of an existing social order. Implicitly or explicitly a project usually constitutes some macro-environments that it treats as unchangeable' (p. 273). The institutional entrepreneurs in this case focused on restructuring the flow of information within the organization rather than bringing about radical changes in work processes. This would have been more difficult to affect as they would require the approval of the ULB's Council (comprising elected representatives) and the state government because the regulations constituting the ULB would have to be modified. Institutional entrepreneurs, therefore, focused on changing the perception that accounting is a terminal function. They promoted an enterprise approach where the Finance Department becomes a service department, acting as a conduit for the informational needs of all other departments in the ULB. They turned their attention to creating new financial management regulations because none existed and adopted an incremental approach to institutional change. Rather can walk in with a plug and play system, undertake organization-wide training on an intensive scale, and insist that the system be used from day one, the institutional entrepreneurs tried a different approach. Changes were introduced in an incremental manner moving from getting the staff to understand their organizational roles and responsibilities to creating a classification system that would streamline data structuring. This was followed by ensuring that staff was first familiarized with this system in a manual form. Next came training them to use the new system while allowing the old system to run alongside. Once staff expressed a degree of comfort with the new system, the old one was terminated. Finally, via directives from the senior management, efforts were made to ensure that the system was used on a regular basis. This incremental approach to reform served to appease any fears that the project would bring about radical changes. In doing so it made F-MIS and PROOF a feasible reform strategy.

The point to note is that the process of financial management was first embedded in practice before the use of the technology. The institutional entrepreneurs felt that technology was merely a tool and it would be easy to get the staff to use it once they understood the logic behind the technology. This approach is different from other such initiatives in India such as the Bhoomi project where the emphasis was on designing the software and the focus was on training the staff in the land records department of the state government to use the software from the day it was installed. The ULB staff gained a high degree of familiarity with how the F-MIS would operate by using the paper-based templates designed by the institutional entrepreneurs. Together with cleaning up the accounting practice and repositioning the finance department, the use of the paper-based templates helped institutionalize the technologically enabled F-MIS because the practices were already in place. Even if F-MIS was to fall by the wayside (due to data entry issues), the institutional entrepreneurs' intent would be served. Another strategy that worked well for the institutional entrepreneurs was juxtaposing the old and the new templates. By running the old accounting system in parallel with F-MIS, the institutional entrepreneurs were able to 'simultaneously make the new structure understandable and accessible, while pointing to potential problems or shortcomings of past practices' (Lawrence & Suddaby, 2005, p. 217).

The temporal sequencing of events—dividing the project in two phases, with the first phase focusing on internal reforms and the second being concerned with creating citizen demand for information—also highlights the attempt by institutional entrepreneurs to create a path that would ensure the institutionalization of their project. Hence, for them, it was logical that the first phase of any project that sought to establish financial accountability must be a project like F-MIS where information flow within the organization is restructured so that it can be accessed by various stakeholders. Once in place, citizen participation could be garnered through campaigns like PROOF. Disclosure forums like PROOF, and training the public to understand and analyze the financial information being generated by F-MIS, established a feedback mechanism. Even if the system faltered due to entropy, the institutional entrepreneurs hoped that the demand from the public for standardized financial documents would make the organization snap out of that state. Also by making F-MIS and its outputs available to the public via PROOF and media reports, the institutional entrepreneurs made it much harder for the ULB to drop the system. If they dropped it, they would have to answer to the public.

By interpreting concerns citizens expressed with regard to corruption as a need for greater transparency and accountability, institutional entrepreneurs conceived of citizens playing the role of auditors. The public might or might not have cared for this role. Similarly, institutional entrepreneurs fixed the role that elected representatives would play. By confining their role to that of an observer, institutional entrepreneurs tried to bypass the existing accountability structures. Not only were the elected representatives left out of the F-MIS project, they were not seen as integral to the PROOF campaign either. It has been pointed out that PROOF was more 'attuned' to working with bureaucrats (Vijayalakshmi, 2004). The PROOF team went to great lengths to establish a working relationship with the bureaucracy, although they knew that this would curtail achieving accountability through the elected representatives (Vijayalakshmi, 2004). This view of accountability stemmed from a feeling that it was easier to work with bureaucrats rather than elected representatives, and some within the campaign were of the view that 'because the officials can be influenced through their contacts with state level politicians (particularly the Chief Minister), it is more sensible for the campaign to have a partnership with the officials' (Vijayalakshmi, 2004, p. 20).

The exclusion of elected representatives from PROOF had its fallouts. The elected representatives felt that the campaign was misguiding the public on the financial management practices within the ULB. The result was that the ULB Council passed a unanimous resolution asking the Commissioner to review of the activities of the PROOF. As a way to win over the elected representatives, PROOF invited the Mayor of the city and other representatives from the ULB Council's Standing Committee on Taxation to attend the PROOF meetings. Attempts were made to meet with selected representatives who were known to be popular and have them advocate for F-MIS and PROOF. This reflects Garud and Karnoe's (2001) finding that, 'to the extent that they are unable to gain momentum with their own approaches, path creation requires an ability on the part of entrepreneurs to shift their emphasis to alternate approaches that may have greater promise' (p. 7).

To ensure that the paths they have created remain stable, institutional entrepreneurs engage in what Lawrence and Suddaby (2005) call 'enabling work'. This refers to the creation of rules that facilitate, supplement, and support institutions. This may include the creation of new roles needed to carry on institutional routines, such as creating the post of the Additional Commissioner of Finance within the ULB, or diverting resources required to ensure institutional survival, and ensuring compliance through enforcement, auditing, and monitoring (Lawrence & Suddaby, 2005). Institutional entrepreneurs use rule making as a means to ensure that the practices they are propagating become institutionalized. Rule making serves a dual purpose: it grants legitimacy to an activity as well as ensures its diffusion. By becoming widely diffused, over time, practices become habitual and are taken for granted (Hwang & Powell, 2006). In the case of the F-MIS project, the passing of the Accounts Regulation reflects this attempt by institutional entrepreneurs. The non-existence of any accounting regulation gave the institutional entrepreneurs an opportunity to carve out a document that reflected all that they considered important and paramount to good financial management. The creation of the F-MIS manual is another attempt to 'actively infuse the normative foundations into the participants' day to day routines and organizational practices' (Lawrence & Suddaby, 2005, p. 233).

CONCLUSION

In summary, we cannot afford to ignore the work of institutional entrepreneurs. They create 'social entanglements' (Selznick, 1996) by embedding ICTs such as F-MIS 'in networks of interdependence, thereby limiting options' (p. 271). By tying F-MIS to internal decision-making processes, finance functions, organizational hierarchy, the existing decentralized administrative setup, disclosure platforms, and financial aid conditionality, institutional entrepreneurs set in motion an inertial momentum which in its own right would contribute to the institutionalization of the new regime. The insights that this case has been able to provide regarding institutionalization also serves to elaborate on the adoption of technological innovations. Many, such as Fountain's (2001a & b) Technology Enactment Model, assume that the process of institutionalization is automatic. However, the F-MIS case highlights the deliberate strategies and tactics used by institutional entrepreneurs to embed practices such that their reproduction is self-activating, occurring through routinized action (Jepperson, 1991).

ACKNOWLEDGMENTS

This chapter builds on an article I co-published in *Journal of Information Technology and Politics* (see Mundkur, Anuradha, & Venkaesh, Murali, 2009) in which we highlighted how diverse stakeholders, by tapping into existing notions of good governance, articulated a project that emphasized reforming financial management systems as fundamental to transforming the working of urban local governments.

NOTES

1. In order to maintain anonymity I will not be identifying the organization but will simply refer to the organization in question as the *ULB*. Its assigned obligatory functions include the maintenance of roads, street lights, sanitation, water supply, registration of births and deaths, public immunizations, and regulation of buildings, and the discretionary functions comprise formation and maintenance of parks, schools, libraries, and hospitals.
2. This section has been drawn from an earlier article: Mundkur, A., & Venkatesh, M. (2009). The role of institutional logics in the design of e-governance systems. *Journal of Information Technology and Politics, 6*(1), 12–30.
3. A division of a city for administrative and representative purposes.

REFERENCES

Asian Development Bank. (1995). *Good governance: Sound development management*. Manila, Philippines: Author. Retrieved January 1, 2007, from www.adb. org/documents/policies/governance/govpolicy.pdf

Benbasat, I., & Zmud, R. W. (2003). The identity crisis within the IS discipline: Defining and communicating the discipline's core principles. *MISQ, 27*(2), 183–194.

Benford, R. D., & Snow, D. A. (2000). Framing processes and social movements: An overview and assessment. *Annual Review of Sociology, 26,* 11–39.

Benjamin, S., & Bhuvaneswari, R. (2001). *Democracy, inclusive governance, and poverty in Bangalore* (Working Paper No. 26). Birmingham, UK: University of Birmingham, School of Public Policy, International Development Department.

Boston, J., Martin, J., Pallot, J., & Walsh, P. (1996). *Public management: The New Zealand model.* Auckland, New Zealand: Oxford University Press.

Colomy, P. (1998). Neofunctionalism and neoinstitutionalism: Human agency and interest in institutional change. *Sociological Forum, 13*(2), 265–300.

Fligstein, N. (1997). Social skill and institutional theory. *American Behavioral Scientist, 40*(4), 397–405.

Fountain, J. (2001a). *Building the virtual state: Information technology and institutional change.* Washington, DC: Brookings Institution Press.

Fountain, J. (2001b). The virtual state: Transforming American government. *National Civic Review, 90*(3), 241–251.

Frumkin, P., & Kaplan, G. (2000). *Neo-institutional theory and the micro-macro link* (Working Paper). Cambridge, MA: Harvard University, Kennedy School of Government.

Garud, R., & Karnoe, P. (2001). Path creation as a process of mindful deviation. In R. Garud & P. Karnøe (Eds.), *Path dependence and creation* (1–36). London: Erlbaum.

Ghosh, A. (2005, November 19). Public-private or a private public? Promised partnership of the Bangalore Agenda Task Force. *Economic and Political Weekly.*

Grand, S., & MacLean, D. (2003). *Creative destruction and creative action: Path dependence and path creation in innovation and change.* Paper presented at the 19th EGOS Colloquium, Copenhagen, Denmark.

Hafeez, S. (2004). *The UN Global E-Government Survey 2004: Towards access for opportunity.* New York: United Nations.

Heeks, R. (2001). *Understanding e-governance for development* (i-Government Working Paper No. 11). Manchester, UK: Institute for Development Policy and Management.

Hood, C. (1995). Contemporary public management: A new global paradigm? *Public Policy and Administration,* 10(2), 104–117.

Hwang, H., & Powell, W. W. (2006). Institutions and entrepreneurship. In S. A. Alvarez, R. Agarwal, & O. Sorenson (Eds.), *Handbook of entrepreneurship research: Disciplinary perspectives* (pp. 179–210). New York: Springer.

Ingraham, P. (1997). Play It Again, Sam; It's Still Not Right: Searching for the Right Notes in Administrative Reform. *Public Administration Review,* 57(4), 325–342.

Jepperson, R. L. (1991). Institutions, institutional effects, and institutionalism. In W. W. Powell & P. J. DiMaggio (Eds.), *The new institutionalism in organizational analysis* (pp. 143–163). Chicago: University of Chicago Press.

Lawrence, T., & Suddaby, R. (2005). Institutions and institutional work. In S. R. Clegg, C. Hardy, T. Lawrence, & W. R. Nord (Eds.), *Handbook of organization studies* (2nd ed., pp. 215–254). Thousand Oaks, CA: Sage.

Mundkur, A., & Venkatesh, M. (2009). The role of institutional logics in the design of e-governance systems. *Journal of Information Technology and Politics,* 6(1), 12–30.

Narayan, G., Nerurkar, A. N., & Mehta, S. J. (2006). Value-proposition of e-governance services: Bridging rural-urban digital divide in developing countries. *International Journal of Education and Development using Information and Communication Technology,* 2(3), 33–44.

NIUA. (2004). Best practices by urban local bodies in India. *Urban Finance,* 7(2), 6–11.

Nye, J. (2001). Information technology and democratic governance. In E. Kamarck & J. S. Nye (Eds.), *Democracy.com? Governance in a networked world* (pp. 1–18). Hollis, NH: Hollis Publishing.

Prayag, A. (2004, July 2). Accountability mantra. The Hindu Business Line. Retrieved November 9, 2011, from http://www.thehindubusinessline.in/life/2004/07/02/stories/2004070200170400.htm

Sachdeva, S. (2002, December). *E-governance strategy in India* (White Paper). Retrieved January 1, 2006, from www.indiaegov.org/knowledgeexchg/egov_strategy.pdf

Selznick, P. (1996). Institutionalism 'old' and 'new'. *Administrative Science Quarterly,* 41(2), 270–277.

Stone-Sweet, A., Fligstein, N., & Sandholtz, W. (2001). The institutionalization of European Space. In A. Stone-Sweet, N. Fligstein, & W. Sandholtz (Eds.), *The institutionalization of Europe* (pp. 1–29). Oxford, UK: Oxford University Press.

Vijayalakshmi, V. (2004). *Fiscal performance audit: Public Record of Operations and Finance (PROOF) and citizens' participation* (IDS Working Paper). Brighton, UK: University of Sussex.

Vithayathil, T. (2004). Reforming municipal financial management systems. *Public Eye*, 6–7.

Winner, L. (1986). *The whale and the reactor: A search for limits in an age of high technology.* Chicago: University of Chicago Press.

Part III

International Development

Critical Perspectives on Health, Poverty, and Environment

International development around the world is fraught with many challenges in a new century. However, international development agendas resemble past goals and motives which largely represent the ongoing accumulation of wealth among the economically powerful regions of the world. Developing communities are less fortunate and continue to play the traditional subservient roles by either producing cheap labour, bartering their land for food or even having to pick scraps form the dumpsters to survive. Human development is not a priority in international development and while the world's growing populations go hungry and deprived, the world's wealthy continue to stock their grocery cupboards and pantries as if they are on the brink of famine.

Bains analyses the practical implications of the Millenium Goals to eradicate hunger and poverty. She claims that unless food production is increased in an environmentally friendly way and unless the wealthy nations take responsibility for the production of food through good agricultural practices, the world's poor will not be fed and the Millennium goal will not be met. Sooknanan and Goorahoo contend that the notion of a sustainable environment in any development initiative suggests that man is in harmony with nature which is not true. They support the call for establishing a sustainable economy. Hemming and Rigney interrogate the notion of Indigenous land use and cultural mapping as a technology of power. Their discussion clearly suggests that digital cultural mapping of a people and their land and waters is yet another Western and colonial legacy to obliterate their real life experiences by retelling their stories from a master's voice perspective and to relocate them to a virtual space. The co-editors conclude the book with a final summary chapter that highlights the key proposals from each chapter and presents these as feasible solutions and options for developing and growing a sustainable future.

9 Food Security
Eliminating Global Poverty and Hunger

Kiran Bains

INTRODUCTION

The United Nations, nearly 60 years ago, proclaimed the Universal Declaration of Human Rights. Some rights, like the 'Right to Food', are overshadowed by those who have received more political and public support, yet severe food insecurity affects one seventh of world's human population. If food production is studied *within* continents and countries, the picture is dismal. However, when food production *across* countries is examined, the availability appears to be enough if distribution of food grain across countries is made in an equitable manner. Nevertheless, such a proposition may not be feasible owing to several political, geographical, economical, and religious considerations. Therefore, each country has to look for attaining self-sufficiency instead to hope for help from food surplus countries. The International Food Policy Research Institute (IFPRI) has forecasted severe food shortage not only in underdeveloped and developing countries but also in developed countries as well. It is now apparent that developed countries like the United States, Russia, and France have been facing acute food shortages in recent years. This has arisen because of putting land to various non-food crops at the cost of food crops. A host of factors have adversely affected production and productivity of food grains in the globe today. Global warming, rocketing oil prices and rapid population explosion have plunged world population into biggest crises in the 21st century by pushing up food prices, spreading hunger and poverty. The fallacy is over 62 nations of the world enjoying fairly good industrial growth are food insecure today mainly because they did not put more emphasis on agriculture. The economic security of developing nations will continue to be predicted based upon the agricultural sector in future. Rapid industrialization at the cost of agriculture may not be rewarding in the long run. A nation's first priority should be to produce food for its citizens and feed and fodder for animals. The developed countries need to reorient their policies. All the countries irrespective of social and political differences must come forward to challenge the global food crises for achieving food security.

A steady growth of population has necessitated that agricultural productivity be enhanced, and this calls for the generation of far more efficient technologies to increase farm productivity, minimum production doses through risk management, diversification, processing, value addition, and commercialization. Excellence of research in frontier areas like biotechnology, nana-technology, molecular biology, geographical information system (GIS), and systems analysis as applied to agriculture will play a pivotal role in attaining food security. It is well recognized that food security relates to access by all people at all times to enough food for an active healthy life. Increased food grain, oilseeds, horticulture, and livestock production as well as food production from the sea through technological interventions, judicial utilization, and eco-friendly intensification in developing countries may add to food security (FAO, 2006a).

Food is a basic requirement of every living being. The landmass available on which food is produced on this earth has been shrinking. The supply of land is fixed and is likely to fall further owing to a wide range of natural and man-made disasters. It is projected that global population will further increase by one billion more by the end of 2050, which will necessitate additional food grains to feed this population. This is not an impossible task, provided the arable lands available in the world are exclusively put under food grains and fodder. The possibility of food grain production is substantial in Asian and African countries. But crops alone may not be able to meet the total requirement unless other sources like the seas and oceans are explored (Clay, 2003).

FOOD SECURITY AT GLOBAL LEVEL

Food security essentially means that all people at all times have access to safe and nutritious food to maintain a healthy and active life (FAO, 1983). This definition implies three dimensions to food security, namely availability, access, and stability at various levels of aggregation, that is, global, national, household, and the individual. The need for food security arises primarily due to the fluctuations in food production, non-availability of sufficient food from domestic sources, and the inability of people to acquire the required amount and composition of foods. The importance of maintaining food security the world over has been abundantly recognized for long. The necessity of having food security at a global level was first recognized at the 1974 World Food Conference where the Food and Agricultural Organization (FAO) of the United Nations was called upon to establish a committee on World Food Security so as to keep the world food situation under constant review and to recommend any action necessary in case of problems in particular areas. Subsequently, the International Undertaking on World Food Security was set up in which member nations committed themselves to food stocks at levels necessary to ensure continuity of supplies and to meet emergency needs in the event of crop failure or natural disaster. Monitoring of implementation of the undertaking has since then become the responsibility of the Committee on World Food Security (CFS, 2005).

Many countries experience perpetual food shortages and distribution problems, which results in chronic and widespread hunger among significant numbers of people. Human populations' exposure to chronic hunger and malnutrition results in decreased body size, also known as stunted growth. This process starts *in utero* if the mother is malnourished and continues through childhood. It leads to higher infant and child mortality rates. Stunted individuals suffer a far higher rate of disease and illness. Severe malnutrition in early childhood often leads to defects in cognitive development. The Asian and African countries are going to be seriously affected unless serious efforts are made to address the high growth of population and fall in productivity. In Asia, a population of 92.7 million of stunted children is due to malnutrition and undernourishment. FAO (2005), UN/SCN (2004), and micronutrient initiative and UNICEF (2005) data expressed that 0.9 billion people worldwide suffer from chronic hunger, 126 million children are underweight, whereas micronutrient deficiencies are prevailing in more than 2 billion of the world population. In year 2000, world leaders committed themselves to the Millennium Development Goals (MDGs). The leaders committed themselves to spare no effort to free their fellow men, women, and children from the abject and dehumanizing conditions of extreme poverty. These goals were framed to function in an integrated way to achieve food and nutrition security. In pursuing these goals, the elimination of hunger, poverty, and maternal and child malnutrition should be the top priorities. An emphasis on healthy, productive individuals means that food security must be attended not simply at the aggregate level but to nutrition security that addresses economic, physical, social, and environmental access to a balanced diet and clean drinking water at the individual level of child, woman, and man. Interpretation of the MDGs must therefore be modified to promote reduction in the absolute number of people living in unsuitable conditions across all countries rather than a reduction in global proportions (Von Braun et al, 2003).

MILLENIUM DEVELOPMENT GOAL—
ERADICATE HUNGER

Of the eight MDGs, the first is to eradicate poverty and hunger and emphasizes a reduction by half the proportion of people who suffer from hunger between 1990 and 2050. The goal to eradicate extreme hunger and poverty depends most on agriculture. Understanding of the ways in which hunger and poverty interconnect and how agriculture can alter the situation are shown in Figures 9.1 and 9.2.

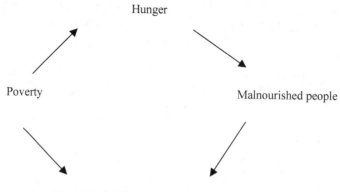

Hunger

Poverty

Malnourished people

Diminished ability to learn, work and care

Figure 9.1   Vicious cycle of hunger and poverty.

Increased agricultural productivity

Healthy people

Better purchasing power/more food

Better Food/care options

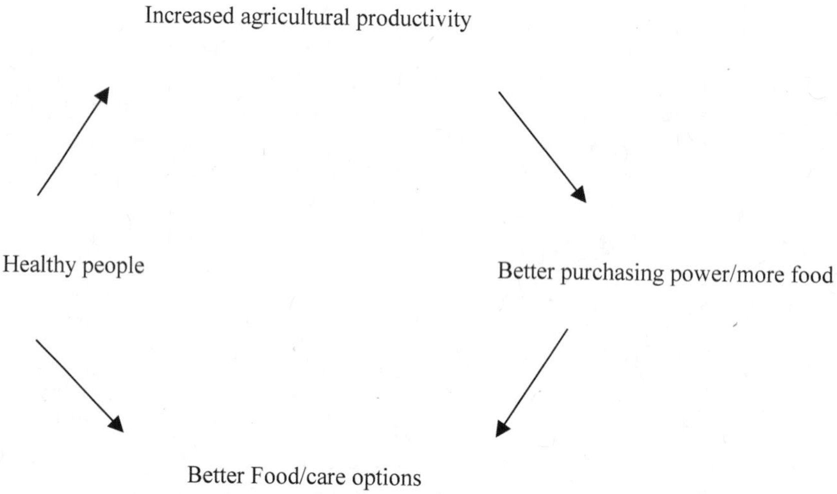

Figure 9.2   Virtuous cycle of hunger and poverty.

In 2005, almost 1.4 billion people lived below poverty line, earning less than $1.25 per day. A projection show that 600 million people in the developing world will suffer from hunger in 2015, 900 million people will continue to live in absolute poverty, and 125 million preschool children will be malnourished. An alternative set of projections indicates that with the proper investments and policies, poverty and hunger can be reduced at a faster rate.

The human right to food is established in many international treaties and other instruments, including the Universal Declaration of Human Rights (1948), the International Covenant on Economics, Social and Cultural

Rights (ICESCR, 1966) and the Convention on the Rights of the Child (1989). Thus the rights-based approach to food security has a legal dimension in that governments have a legal obligation to enable all individuals within their borders not merely to be free from hunger but to produce or procure, in ways that are fully consistent with their human dignity, food that is adequate for an active and healthy life. The rights require 'the availability of food in a quantity and quality sufficient to satisfy the dietary needs of individuals free from adverse substances and acceptable within a given culture; the accessibility of such food in ways that are sustainable and they do not interfere with the enjoyment of other human rights' (ICESCR, 1999). It is the right to feed oneself in dignity rather than the right to be fed. By recognizing the Right to Food, governments have an obligation to respect, protect, and fulfill this right enabling them to achieve the objective of World Food Summit and first millennium goal of reducing hunger by 2015.

The human right to food declares that every individual is a rights-holder, fully entitled to demand that the state perform these duties. A rights-based approach views governments' promotion of food security as an obligation, not as a form of benevolence. It insists on the accountability of duty-bearers to rights-holders. Furthermore, it is important not only that the state recognizes all individuals as right-holders but also that individuals see themselves in the same way and are able to act accordingly. In short, every individual must be empowered, and this empowerment is the state's obligation.

If a nation is genuinely to treat adequate food for all as a human right, and if it is determined to make that right a reality for each individual, what must it do?

States must realize that they have the obligation

- not to deprive anyone of access to adequate food;
- to protect everyone from being deprived of such access in any other way; and
- to proactively create an environment where people become self-reliant for food or, where people are unable to do so, to ensure that food is provided.

Governments can achieve the first goal by (1) establishing stronger, more knowledgeable voices among both duty-bearers and right-holders to ensure accurate targeting, accessible justice, effective action, and durable impact and thus contribute profoundly to sustainable development and the achievement of the MDGs. (2) All individuals have an equal right to food, but people's differing circumstances mean that different actions are required by the government for the right to be realized for all situations arising out of conflicts and other disasters require special protection and support measures. A right-based approach demands that those who are the most vulnerable be identified and empowered to claim their rights. It demands and corrects any discriminatory processes in governance and power structure. (3) The degree of a state's commitment to the progressive realization of the human right to food can be observed from the development and implementation of policies to monitoring and evaluation. Policies so designed should take care of tackling the underlying reasons of vulnerability as well as support the empowerment of those affected, providing them with the tools to claim their rights. (4) Durable impact needs to be studied. For this, realistic targets should be identified and benchmarks should be formulated. Right-based monitoring means monitoring not just the outcomes but also the structures and processes (FAO 2006b and 2006c).

MILLENIUM DEVELOPMENT GOALS—FROM EDUCATION TO GLOBAL PARTNERSHIP FOR DEVELOPMENT

The second millennium goal is to achieve universal primary education. To achieve this goal for education we must take into account education's link to agriculture and food and nutrition security. Poor rural households often cannot afford to send their children to school. Education fees and the opportunity costs of educating children, rather than putting them to work to earn money or help at home or on the farm, can be prohibitive. It therefore takes a three-pronged strategy to address this huge trade-off: (1) food for children in school; (2) incentives (food or cash) for parents and support services (crèches) for working mothers so that they can send children to school; and (3) improvements in agricultural productivity and market functioning to ensure adequate food supply and access.

The third millennium goal is to promote gender equality and empower women. Many women are farmers. But unlike men, who have greater opportunities for non-agricultural work, women mainly depend upon agriculture to secure food or earn money for their families. Improvements in agriculture, therefore, can contribute in a fundamental way to increasing incomes and economically empowering women.

The links between agriculture and child mortality are indirect but important. About half of all deaths occur because of malnutrition, which prevents children from fighting off even common childhood ailments. Mildly underweight children are twice are likely to die prematurely as children who have normal weight. The risk of dying increases five- to eight-fold for children who are moderately or severely malnourished. The absence of essential micronutrients further exacerbates poor children's vulnerability to disease.

Improving maternal health is another goal. To properly care for their children, women need to be healthy. Self-reliant educated women with access to adequate resources are better able to care for themselves. Thus meeting the goal for education and women's empowerment by improving agricultural productivity can indirectly improve women's health.

Combating HIV/AIDS, malaria, and other diseases is the sixth goal and requires a holistic perspective. A dynamic agricultural sector can reduce risky economic behavior, increase the demand for education and good health care, and provide adequate food for leading a healthy life and fighting illness if the need arises. The spreading HIV/AIDS epidemic has quickly become a major obstacle in the fight against hunger and poverty in developing countries. Food production has dropped dramatically in countries with high HIV/AIDS prevalence rates. Moreover, without proper food and nutrition, people living with HIV will transition to AIDS more rapidly, because individuals with HIV require up to 50% more protein and up to 15% more calories than healthy individuals. The incidence of tuberculosis (TB) is also associated with malnutrition and poverty. People who lack appropriate diets and access to essential micronutrients, such as iron, vitamin D, and zinc are more likely to contract tuberculosis and to progress faster from infection to active TB and early death. To attain the MDG for disease, the resources of the agricultural sector need to be coordinated with those of the health sector to meet the joint challenges of poverty reduction and disease reduction.

In the seventh goal, the millennium declaration targets a variety of environmental issues such as biodiversity, critical natural habitats, energy use, global climate change, safe water and sanitation, and urban slums. A productive agricultural sector can reduce pressure in all of these areas. In fact, many agricultural practices that push productivity tend to do so at the expense of the environment. Pressure to increase agricultural production with inappropriate policies in the past have resulted in soil degradation, greater concentration of greenhouse gases in the atmosphere, marine pollution, overexploitation of fisheries, and loss of valuable habitats. People who suffer from food and nutrition insecurity generally try to safeguard their environments but often fail for lack of resources and the capacity to organize the needed collective action at the local level.

The eighth and final MDG is to develop a global partnership for development. Wrestling with the problems of development is going to require countries to work together closely at the regional and international levels to address a wide range of issues. Creating jobs for young people and institutional conditions that facilitate agricultural development can make a strong contribution to achieve this goal. Although initially the jobs created will be within agriculture, once general economic growth kicks in as a result of agricultural growth, employment opportunities will arise in other sectors.

CONCLUSION

World economic security will continue to be predicted based upon the agriculture sector in future. A steady growth in population has necessitated that agricultural productivity be enhanced for meeting the requirement by

2050. Higher agricultural productivity will require seeds and other agricultural technologies which need to match local agro climatic, labor, and market needs of small-scale farmers. These technologies must be environmental friendly and should come from both conventional and newer scientific approaches, including scientifically sound and environmentally safe genetic modification.

REFERENCES

Clay E. (2003). Food security: Concepts and measurement Chap. 2 in *Trade and food security: Conceptualizing the linkages.* Rome: FAO.

Committee on World Food Security (CFS). (2005). *Assessment of the world food security situation.* Rome: FAO.

Food and Agriculture Organization (FAO). (1983). *World food security: A reappraisal of the concepts and approaches* (Director-general's report). Rome: Author.

FAO. (2006a). *Food security* (Policy Brief, Issue 2). FAO Agriculture and Development Economics Division.

FAO. (2006b). *The right to food guidelines.* Rome: Author.

FAO. (2006c). *The right to food in practice: Implementation at the national level.* Rome: Author.

ICESCR (1999). The right to adequate food (Art. 11). General Comments E/C .12/1999/5. The International Covenant on Economics, Social and Cultural Rights.

Von Braun, J., Swaminathan, M. S., & Rosegrant, M. W. (2003). *2003–2004 IFPRI annual report essay: Agriculture, food security, nutrition and the millennium development goals.* Washington, DC: International Food Policy Research Institute.

10 The Race Toward Green Energy and Sustainable Development

Prahalad Sooknanan and Anil Goorahoo

INTRODUCTION

Since the beginning of time, humans have always strived for survival. This struggle is even more evident today, given the alarming regularity of natural disasters such as tsunamis, volcanoes, earthquakes, and floods. While these can be attributed to the forces of nature, humans continue to be their worst enemies, contributing wittingly and unwittingly to pollution which has assumed global proportions. This threat has far-reaching implications particularly for developing countries as they strive to satisfy basic needs such as potable water, utilities, and food. These efforts have been supported by ongoing individual and collective attempts at innovations in minimizing waste, improving technology, using resources more efficiently, and legislating against pollution. Notwithstanding, these initiatives often result in further ecological costs. In other words, even the best intentions have not been sympathetic to the ideal of sustainability, which is essentially the power to sustain future generations without compromising their quality of life.

Fundamentally, the notion of a sustainable world is premised on harmony between human activities and the natural environment. To this end, the key human ingredient is economic activity and its symbiotic relationship with the natural environment. Today, however, the impact of humans on the natural environment mitigates any possibility of sustainable development, rendering future economic development in jeopardy. Consequently, this environment of ignorance and insecurity warrants the intervention of the world community and its specialized agencies.

The response to this clarion call is to develop a sustainable global economy. According to Dorf (2001), a sustainable global economy is one that the earth is capable of sustaining indefinitely. Dorf shares the growing anxiety that depletion of the natural resources and increasing pollution may overcome the planet's capabilities. In other words, humans may be destroying the ability of future generations to meet their basic needs for daily survival. In more practical terms, Daly (1996) deems a sustainable economy as one in which the rates of renewable resources do not exceed regeneration rates. He emphasizes that the rates of non-renewable resources must not exceed rates of development of renewable substitutes. Further, the rates of pollution must not exceed assimilative capacities of the environment. To this end, development initiatives must cover the need for environmental unity, which implies that environments are so linked that what is done in one region is likely to affect other regions and eventually the entire planet. This ideal is consistent with the concept of a sustainable ecosystem, which ensures that when a resource is harvested, it must still be able to maintain its essential functions and properties (Botkin & Keller, 1998).

At a general level, the concept of a sustainable economy is grounded in the interrelationship among economic viability, environmental quality, and social justice (Dorf, 2001). These three conditions for a sustainable economy are inextricably linked, and none can be attained without necessary attention to all. Inevitably, this scenario provokes controversy among environmentalists, entrepreneurs, development advocates, and governments as to which of the three deserves more attention. In the end, however, the fundamental concern remains sustainability, which is generally viewed as the ability to meet current and future needs while maintaining a good quality of life. Consistent with this view, it is imperative that a sustainable world provide goods and services (outputs) using a set of inputs to provide a good quality of life while sustaining the ecological basis for this activity (Daly, 1996). It is important to note, however, that while consensus for ideals such as quality of life and sustainability is elusive, the ideal of a good life remains a utopian dream.

Notwithstanding the many strategies touted for resolving this environmental conflict and attaining the dream of a quality life, much attention has been focused on the increasing threat of global warming and the greenhouse effect. Scientists continue to caution the build-up of 'greenhouse gases' that can potentially destabilize the atmosphere. These gases include carbon dioxide, methane, and nitrous oxide. On the other hand, emissions from automobile and industrial plants cause the atmosphere temperature to increase which results in 'global warming'. Indeed, recent upheavals in the global weather patterns such as floods and heat waves have contributed to the build-up of carbon dioxide in the earth's atmosphere. It is, therefore, evident that a solution to this global challenge is of urgent importance. To this end, one potential solution is to embrace and implement steps toward 'green energy' particularly by developing countries.

In the past, and particularly during the Industrial Revolution, resources were believed to be infinite. Natural resources were used in abundance to manufacture products for human consumption. Today, however, it has dawned on manufacturers that they have to abandon traditional ways of production to ensure sustainability in the long run. For instance, there is a current trend toward a cleaner model for manufacturing and business practices as a whole. The aim is to revolutionize human industry from the traditional mindset and mode of production into a system that facilitates the integration of economic, environmental, and ethical considerations.

According to Dorf (2001), 'the goal of this cleaner model of industrialization is to release less pollution, think long term, reduce regulations, produce fewer toxic materials, reduce wastes, and improve the condition of the earth's ecosystem' (p. 109).

The present model of industrialization therefore advocates an economy that facilitates a cyclic use of materials. In other words, whereas waste was seen as simply discarded by-products or emissions from individual products, processes, or service operations, there is now a more conscious effort to utilize waste as actual by-products and recycled materials as goods for human consumption notwithstanding the inherent challenges of waste disposal that can still become compostable. Indeed, this approach is consistent with the concept of 'eco-efficiency', or the state of delivering competitively priced goods and services while reducing ecological impacts within the limits of the earth's 'carrying capacity', which is the earth's ability to provide inputs for a given level of human use over time. Within this framework, the aim is to produce more from less material and energy in keeping with Fussler's (1996) goal of cutting the current energy and materials flows by one-half. Overall, according to DeSimone and Popoff (1997), 'eco-efficiency' should help to reduce costs and liabilities associated with resource consumption, waste, and pollution.

In an attempt to achieve eco-efficiency through environmental design, Fiskel (1996) highlights a new practice being adopted by companies called Design for Environment (DFE), which is a systematic consideration of environmental performance during the early stage of product development. It is therefore not surprising that manufacturers are always creating innovative solutions in response to customer needs, industry regulations, and market forces. To this end, Porter (1995) states that if environmental standards are properly designed, they can trigger innovations that have the potential to lower the total cost of a product or improve its value. These innovations in turn will allow companies to use a range of inputs from raw materials to energy to labor more productively, thus offsetting the costs of improving environmental impact and ending the stalemate. Porter (1995) further argues that this enhanced *resource productivity* makes companies more competitive, not less.

GREEN ENERGY

Consistent with the objective of DFE to design safe and eco-efficient products and services, the designing of *green products* is currently being advocated. Essentially, green products meet one or more of the qualities of eco-efficiency and distinguish themselves from their competitors through labeling and advertising terms such as *biodegradable, compostable, environmentally friendly,* or *organic*. More specifically, Conway-Schempf and Lave (1996) define a green product as one that uses fewer materials and less energy in its production, use, and disposal than other products of similar function (particularly less non-renewable resources). They also note that green products use fewer toxic materials or result in lower discharges of hazardous materials than other products. According to these authors, it is evident that the substitution of green products for less environmentally conscious products is a step toward preserving the environment and giving future generations the same opportunities we enjoy, an ideal they describe as *sustainable economic development.*

In spite of the merits of green products, Hendrickson and McMichael (1992) emphasize that product design is fundamental to addressing environmental problems. In other words, in the design stage, designers must be cognizant of manufacturing decisions, resource requirements, toxic materials usage, energy use, and waste disposal, among other considerations. These considerations are particularly essential for *green manufacturing,* which Atlas and Florida (1998) describe as the practice whereby industrial facilities can implement technologies and workplace practices to improve the environmental outcomes of their production processes. Porter and van der Linde (1995) claim that green manufacturing can lead to lower material costs, production efficiency gains, reduced environmental and occupational safety expenses, and an improved corporate image. Initiatives at green manufacturing and green products can ultimately culminate in *green marketing,* or the advertising and marketing of environmentally sensitive products to convey information and influence consumer choice.

Generally speaking, the goal of *green energy* is to create power in a manner that reduces pollution to a bare minimum, bearing in mind that every mode of energy collection will result in some pollution. With green energy, however, the pollution created is considerably less, prompting advocates of this kind of energy to argue that its widespread use would help reduce production of greenhouse gases, thereby preserving the planet for a much longer time. It is greenhouse gases, that are the by-products of traditional energy sources derived from fossil fuels, which contribute to global warming. By limiting dependency on energy sources that use fossil fuels, it is believed that greenhouse emissions can be reduced enough to dramatically restrict the current rate at which the earth is heating.

Usually references to green energy sources have to do with solar, wind-driven, or hydro power—all of which have proven records for efficiency and cost-effectiveness. Their combined qualities of environmental friendliness and lower production costs make them ideal power sources for countries with the natural resources and technical knowledge to develop these industries. However, even countries that lack abundant natural and financial resources have the opportunity to get on board the green energy revolution through developing strategies in building design and construction. It is possible now to construct buildings in such a way that their architectural designs will help keep them cool during the day and heated at nights. Through this method the need for air-conditioning and heating systems is removed, or considerably reduced, and the building design becomes a source of green energy.

Another method that is gaining popularity in the race toward a less polluted environment is to develop sources of green energy sources nearer the sites where they will be used rather than bringing them in from elsewhere. Electrification of private homes, for example, can be achieved using solar panels that have the capacity to produce excess power, which can be fed back into the regional or national grid to be used elsewhere. It is a method that is seen as having distinct advantages over the establishment of many large power plants, which are producers of massive amounts of greenhouse gases. However, while solar panels represent an attractive option for domestic power supplies, their relatively high set-up cost places them out of the reach of many—particularly in poorer countries with communities in distant locations that may be outside the reach of power grids. Nevertheless, Germany has been pursuing this method with remarkable success.

Among the other strategies being pursued to create green energy sources is development of new technologies that will clean up the processes by which existing fossil fuels are converted into energy. In this way, it is believed the final product can be achieved with only a small fraction of the current amount of pollution. The concept of producing clean coal has gained currency, and studies are currently being done to determine how energy could be harvested from coals and other fossil fuels in a manner that would not produce potentially devastating pollutants.

RACE TO LOW-CARBON EMISSIONS

Today, countries around the world appear to be waking up to the need for safer energy sources and many, including some of the most rapidly developing, countries have set emissions targets within the framework of national climate policies. China and Germany have emerged as leaders in this initiative. Further, the New York University School of Law's Institute for Policy Integrity believes in the not-too-distant future there is going to be a huge market for green energy and the Scandinavian countries and Germany are leading that charge with China quickly catching up.

It is estimated that if all of the 154 existing emission policies are successfully implemented, harmful emissions could decline by 9 gigatons by the year 2020 but that would still be 3 to 5 gigatons less than the target. An emissions reduction of between 12 and 14 gigatons is required to achieve the 'stabilization pathway' that is needed to manage the amount of carbon dioxide in the atmosphere and to keep the rise in global temperature below 2 degrees Celsius.

The biggest contributors so far to the decline in harmful emissions have been identified as Germany and Brazil, with China also playing an important role. China aims to reduce its harmful emissions by 40% to 45% by

2020, below 2005 levels. Brazil has set a target of 20% reduction below 2005 levels by 2020. Together, they will eliminate almost 2 gigatons of harmful emissions. In addition, China emerged in 2009 as the world's largest investor in clean energy, having put more than $34 billion into low-carbon technologies. That is almost twice the figure invested by the United States, but on a per capita basis the investment still falls considerably short of China responsibility. Germany, on the other hand, is way ahead, having long established 'feed-in' tariffs that reward consumers for producing renewable electricity. The excess electricity that is produced is fed back into the grid. A report from Germany's Deutsche Bank describes such 'feed-in' tariffs as an integral underpinning of any prosperous green economy. The Center for American Progress (CAP) estimates that clean energy will be a $2.3 trillion industry by 2020, and China will be right in the middle of it, along with Germany and Spain, which all have multiple national policies. The CAP also maintains that each of these countries has a long-term, sustained plan of how to ramp up clean energy industries and also lower carbon emissions. Today, the current annual investment in the global energy industry stands at approximately US$350 billion, of which more than US$100 billion accounts for renewable energy.

DEVELOPING COUNTRIES AND GREEN ENERGY

It is often said that energy is a key requirement for economic development and that there is a direct correlation between energy consumption and the standard of living. However, in excess of 50% of the world's rural population has no access to modern energy infrastructure. Many developing countries around the world, particularly some within the African continent, enjoy only limited supply from their national grid. Uganda, for example, has a national grid that covers less than 5%. Even those areas which are covered experience frequent load shedding because the power generated is insufficient to satisfy the needs of growing national demand. Under these circumstances, it is not uncommon for electricity to be turned off for several hours at a time. In some instances, the supply is interrupted for days and perhaps months at a time. It is estimated that more than 95% of African countries do not benefit from electricity delivered by their respective national grids and it is not anticipated that the figure will improve in the foreseeable future. The consequence has been retardation of economic and infrastructural development.

For this reason, renewable energy is thought to be the most viable option for most developing countries, particularly in rural and sometimes remote areas where centrally located national grid systems would pose challenges associated with transmission and distribution. Rather, production of green renewable energy through mini power plants, with local distribution capacity over a small area or through solar home systems, appears to offer the most viable option. These mini power plants can make adequate use of free green energy that is both renewable and abundantly available in the form of wind power, solar power, hydro power, bio-fuel, and biomass.

Considerable investment has gone into research and development with a view to making these techniques more efficient and reliable as well as to improve quality. The result has been a dramatic increase in production with a corresponding decline in the cost of renewable energy technologies. To have the desired effect of a green revolution though, these cost savings need to be transferred to developing countries and in June 2009, Director-General of the United Nations Industrial Development Organization (UNIDO) Kandeh K. Yumkella emphasized the need for developed nations to help out their less developed neighbors. He told an International Energy Conference in Vienna that developed nations needed to pay far more attention to promoting use of green energy and to establishing sources of green energy in developing nations.

The global financial and economic crisis which saw the demise of some of the world's biggest institutions toward the end of the first decade of the 21st century is being viewed as the best incentive for countries to pursue a green energy revolution. UNIDO's Director-General described his organization's most important task as helping developing countries rebuild their economies and strengthen support in the promotion of 'green energy revolution for developing countries'. It was a point emphasized by the president of the United Nations Intergovernmental Panel on Climate Change (IPCC), who points out that transformation from current energy sources to renewable energy cannot abandon developing countries.

ENERGY LEAPFROGGING IN TOGO

Some advocates of green energy sources are excited about the possibilities on offer through the absence of fossil fuel energy in many of the world's developing countries. In a process known as 'energy leapfrogging', it is theorized that green energy could be introduced to many of these regions without first establishing energy sources that rely upon fossil fuels. This would speed up the process of electrification and simultaneously establish the infrastructure to provide environment-friendly energy. In Kpalime, Togo, businessman Claude Amouzou-Togo peddles solar energy sources and attracts an average of one customer per month. The low rate of sales is blamed on high set-up costs and almost total absence of government support for renewable energies. Still, there is a lot of business that can be done because much of the region's population is without electricity.

In the absence of a regional grid, particularly in rural villages, solar panels have distinct advantages. Whereas it may take years to connect even one community to a grid, villages can set their own priorities and introduce solar energy to key institutions such as hospitals and schools, saving both time and money in the process because both costs and benefits would be distributed across the village. The process, although challenged by a lack of support from the government, is aided by the involvement of micro-credit organizations which provide loans to cover the relatively large set-up costs. It is hoped that at some stage the government will come on board with the private sector to help bring costs down. As a first step, the state could assist by reducing existing customs taxes, which provide an almost insurmountable cost barrier to importing essential green technologies.

BRAZIL LEADING THE WAY

Despite poverty that threatens to cripple its economy, one of South America's largest countries, Brazil, has emerged as a global leader in developing alternative fuel. Astronomical oil prices of the 1970s forced Brazil to seek out alternative sources of energy, and its vast acreage of sugar cane provided an abundant supply of ethanol. By 1985, the country had the distinction of powering more than 90% of its cars with ethanol derived from sugar cane. It has saved the country billions of dollars that would have been spent importing oil and simultaneously spared the country of the carbon emissions that derives from burning gasoline. In comparison, up to 2006 the use of alternative fuels in the rest of the world was a mere 1%.

At 2009 prices, Brazil had the capacity to produce ethanol for approximately US$1 per gallon equivalent, as compared with the international price of gasoline, which is approximately US$1.50 per gallon. Admittedly, ethanol fuel offers lower mileage than gasoline, but in Brazil the cost per mile driven is still considerably less. Not surprising therefore, 20% of Brazil's transportation market uses ethanol as its main source of fuel. This figure is likely to increase as research into ethanol as a major source of transportation fuel is taking on added significance. Authorities in Brazil have begun collaborating with Japan to expand ethanol research and possibly to pursue new ventures in the area. It is hoped that the United States will become involved through a knowledge sharing program on sustainable renewable energy that will lead eventually to development of more fuel-efficient vehicles.

GREEN ENERGY STRATEGIES

In today's race toward green energy as a means of attaining sustainable development, several strategies have been advanced. One measure proposed for manufacturers to become more responsible about the environment is the concept of *social entrepreneurship,* which involves a combination of social and environmental benefits with traditional business practices as distinct from *economic entrepreneurship,* which is focused on revenues and profits.

The hybrid of social entrepreneurship has in turn spawned the paradigm of *social innovation,* which promotes partnerships between private enterprise and public interest organizations that produce profitable and sustainable change for both parties (Kanter, 1999).

The ultimate goal of sustainable development, however, is to ensure that it attains the Three Es or the 'triple bottom line' of environmental quality, economic health, and social equality. Today, governments have embraced varying options of the principles of the Three Es as they strive to achieve satisfactory standards of sustainability by applying a mix of traditional and innovative approaches to governance. Toward this end, the 1992 United Nations Earth Summit in Rio de Janeiro adopted sustainable development as the principle that should guide the evolution of the world's communities and economies. Seventeen years later, in December 2009, world leaders got together for climate talks in Denmark and agreed on a program called REDD (Reducing Emissions from Deforestation and Degradation), which, within 6 months, raised over US$4 billion. It included a contribution of US$500 million from Germany on the heels of another environmental conference in May 2010, which was convened in Oslo, Norway, to start talks on the creation of a single international agency to monitor and finance efforts to help poorer nations protect their forests and biodiversity. Around the same time, Norway itself pledged US$1 billion, which did not form part of the REDD program, to help fight deforestation in Indonesia, which has become a major emitter of carbon due to logging, crop-growing, and cattle grazing.

At another level, Goklany (2000) notes the argument implicitly or explicitly advanced for making immediate and significant reductions in greenhouse gas emissions, cautioning that human-induced climate change on top of other environmental problems has the potential of overwhelming human and natural systems particularly with respect to natural ecosystems, forests, and biodiversity.

Today, it is becoming increasingly evident that most indicators of human and environmental well-being improve with wealth. To this end, Goklany (2000) argues that the poorer countries in the developing world are hungrier and more malnourished, and their populations continue to strive in an environment of polluted air and water, making them more prone to death and disease from climate-sensitive infections and parasitic diseases resulting in higher mortality rates and lower life expectancies. This is not surprising because these populations are more vulnerable to climate change and particularly because they often lack the necessary resources to adapt adequately. It would therefore be expedient for these countries to enhance their economic growth by embracing technological innovations so as to make their people more resilient and less vulnerable to adversity in general, and to climate change in particular.

At another level, Myers (2000) advocates the revision of consumption patterns in order to achieve all-round sustainability of our economies and lifestyles. To this end, he recommends that the first step toward sustainable consumption is to recognize that consumption patterns will inevitably change in the future through global warming and other environmental problems. This is particularly relevant to the 800 million people in developing countries who should deservedly enjoy a standard of living that transcends the present subsistence level. In this regard, the business sector may help as they are generally perceived as the source of consumption-derived environmental problems. In other words, as Hawken, Lovins, and Lovins (1999) argue, if human communities were to deploy all of the ecotechnologies that are already available from innovative business such as energy efficiency, pollution controls, waste management, recycling, cradle-to-cradle products, and zero-emissions industry, people could potentially enjoy twice as much material welfare while consuming only half as many natural resources and causing only half as much pollution and waste.

CONCLUSION

The need to expedite development of green energy sources in countries of the South has taken on added significance in the wake of projections which clearly show that not only the rate of energy consumption but also the carbon emissions of developing countries are rising at a rapid pace. However, the energy-efficient technologies that currently exist in some industrialized countries may not necessarily be feasible for wholesale transfer to developing regions. Technologies used in the development of green energy sources are still relatively expensive, and it may be necessary for some governments to provide substantial subsidies to encourage their implementation on a large scale. Additionally, some developing countries are handicapped by crippling inefficiencies within their energy infrastructure, which, when combined with problems like lack of awareness and inadequate planning, add to the difficulties associated with implementing these technologies.

It may be necessary therefore to determine, through rigorous 'end-use research', those technologies that may be best suited to any given developing country. Examples of the usefulness of such studies can be found in Turkey and Northern Cyprus. In the case of Turkey, it was demonstrated that transfer of green energy technologies would be more feasible for their industrial sector, whereas in Northern Cyprus technology transfer would yield greatest benefits in the residential and commercial sectors.

REFERENCES

Atlas, M., & Florida, R. (1998). Green manufacturing. In R. Dorf (Ed.), *The Technology Handbook* (13–89). Boca Raton, Florida: CRC Press.

Botkin, D., & Keller, E. (1998). *Environmental science.* New York: Wiley.

Conway-Schempf, N., & Lave, L. (1996, Winter). Pollution prevention through green design. *Pollution Prevention Review,* 11–20.

Daly, H. (1996). *Beyond growth: The economics of sustainable development.* Boston: Beacon Press.

DeSimone, L., & Popoff, F. (1997). *Eco-efficiency.* Cambridge: MA: MIT Press.

Dorf, C. R. (2001). *Technology, humans, and society: Towards a sustainable world.* San Diego, CA: Academic Press.

Fiskel, J. (1996). *Design for environment: Creating eco-efficient products and processes.* New York: McGraw-Hill.

Florida, R., & Atlas, M. (1997). *Report on field research on environmentally-conscious manufacturing in the United States.* Pittsburgh, PA: Carnegie Mellon University.

Fussler, C. (1996). *Driving eco-innovation.* London: Pitman.

Goklany, I. M. (2000). Potential consequences of increasing atmospheric CO_2 concentration compared to other environmental problems. *Technology,* 7(Suppl. 1), 189–213.

Hawken, P., Lovins, A. B., & Lovins, L. H. (1999). *Natural capitalism: The next industrial revolution.* Boston: Little, Brown.

Hendrickson, C. T., & McMichael. F. C. (1992). Product design for the environment. *Environmental Science and Technology, 26,* 844.

Kanter, F. (1999, May–June). From spare change to real change. *Harvard Business Review,* pp. 127–132.

Porter, M. E. (1995, September). Green and competitive. *Harvard Business Review,* pp. 120–133.

Myers, N. (2000). Sustainable consumption. *Science,* Vol. 287, 2419.

Porter, M. E., & van der Linde, C. (1995). Green and competitive: Ending the stalemate. *Harvard Business Review, 73,* 120–134.

11 Indigenous Land Use and Occupancy Mapping as a Technology of Power

Steve Hemming and Daryle Rigney

> The land and waters is a living body.
> We the Ngarrindjeri people are a part of its existence.
> The land and waters must be healthy for the Ngarrindjeri people to be healthy.
> We are hurting for our Country.
> The Land is dying, the River is dying, the Kurangk (Coorong) is dying and the Murray Mouth is closing.
> What does the future hold for us?
>
> Tom Trevorrow (cited in Ngarrindjeri Nation, 2006, p. 4)

> It is man with his planet Earth, with his territory, with his body, who is now the satellite. Once transcendent, he has become exorbitant.
>
> Jean Baudrillard (1993, p. 3)

INTRODUCTION

In this chapter we provide a critical reading of indigenous land use and occupancy mapping, a practice that has emerged from North America and is increasingly being promoted in Australia and across the Pacific Rim. As a 'new' information technology tool it is promoted as an innovative instrument in the safeguarding of cultural diversity and cultural knowledge and an empowering instrument for indigenous self-determination. Indigenous people in the Murray Darling Basin region in southeastern Australia are in the process of negotiating rights to water and natural resources at local, state, and federal levels. In this context, land use and occupancy mapping offers opportunities and potential problems. Our account examines this context at various levels: for the Ngarrindjeri Nation, the traditional owners of the lower River Murray region; for other Indigenous nations in the Murray Darling Basin; and finally Pacific Rim indigenous peoples. We are particularly sensitive to the colonizing tendencies of disciples such as geography and environmental studies when they work in tandem with new technologies and the governments of settler democracies. In this context we raise the issue of 'virtual' subjectivity and draw attention to what we describe as land use and occupancy mapping's hyper colonial characteristics. We argue that critical readings of power relations, and traditionalist constructions of culture and identity, need to inform indigenous decisions about engagement with technologies of power such as indigenous land use and occupancy mapping. A future oriented understanding of culture and tradition is essential for Indigenous engagements with development, but most importantly, the management practices that seek to 'protect' environment and heritage. In adopting a critical reading of use and occupancy mapping we also recognize its potential to assist indigenous leadership in the development of strategic engagements that produce positive transformations, greater recognition of indigenous rights, and improvements in community well-being.

The authors of this chapter are working with Ngarrindjeri elders, leaders, and non-Indigenous colleagues to develop a sustainable, regional Indigenous community/economy based on the Ngarrindjeri ontology of Ruwe/Ruwar[1]—country/body/spirit (Bell, 1998, 2008; Ngarrindjeri Nation, 2006; Hemming & Rigney, 2008). Daryle Rigney is a Ngarrindjeri academic and community leader, and Steve Hemming is a non-Indigenous interdisciplinary researcher. The Ngarrindjeri Nation is located at the bottom end of the River Murray, part of Australia's Murray Darling Basin system, a river system that has been seriously degraded by drought and poor water management practices.

In recent years the Ngarrindjeri have developed a new relationship with all levels of Australian governments—local, state, and federal. This relationship is being built on negotiated recognition of traditional ownership of Ngarrindjeri *Ruwe* (lands and waters) through formal agreements called Kungun Ngarrindjeri Yunnan (KNY 'listen to what Ngarrindjeri people are saying'), the demands created by the environmental degradation of the Murray Darling Basin, and an Indigenous move toward regional governance and self-determination (Bell, 2008; Hemming & Rigney, 2008; Hemming & Trevorrow, 2005).

In response to increasing calls for recognition of Indigenous water rights and greater Indigenous involvement in environmental management, the Murray Darling Basin Authority (MDBA) and the Murray Lower Darling River Indigenous Nations (MILDRIN) alliance are promoting Indigenous use and occupancy mapping as a valuable 'tool' for supporting the 'inclusion' of Indigenous cultural values in natural resource management (MDBA, 2009; Morgan, Weir, & Strelein, 2004; Tobias, 2000, 2010). In its 2008–2009 annual report, the MDBA defines use and occupancy mapping in the following terms:

> Use and occupancy mapping is a survey method for documenting Indigenous peoples' contemporary use of land and water; it is a tool for developing planning and management strategies based on Indigenous peoples' social, cultural and environmental relationships to those areas of usage. The Canadian-devised method has been jointly adopted here in Australia for the first time by MLDRIN and MDBA. (MDBA, 2009)

So far the Ngarrindjeri Nation has had limited involvement in Indigenous use and occupancy mapping and has directed energy and resources into establishing regional governance, negotiating new framework agreements with governments, and developing community-based caring for country and related economic development programs. The authors of this paper have argued for the strategic primacy of Ngarrindjeri management planning documents such as the *Ngarrindjeri Nation Yarluwar-Ruwe Plan* (Ngarrindjeri Nation, 2006), which broadly sets the parameters of Ngarrindjeri interests in lands and waters (Hemming et al., 2007; Hemming & Rigney, 2008). With strong regional Indigenous governance and framework agreements with governments at all levels, Ngarrindjeri are developing the capacity to assess and strategically engage with new technologies and projects such as use and occupancy mapping. We argue that without this core capacity, First Nations are severely disadvantaged in their interactions with the complex bureaucracies and research, business, and policy networks that characterize contemporary settler nation-states.

RESISTING CLOSURE: CULTURAL FUTURES AND NEW TECHNOLOGIES

In southern South Australia, native title and Aboriginal heritage provide some legislative recognition of Indigenous rights to *Ruwe*, but there are no treaties and the legal platform for Indigenous futures is shifting and often tenuous (Hemming, 2006; Rigney, Hemming, & Berg, 2008; Strelein, 2006). In this colonizing legal/political setting, mapping practices have been historically instituted and controlled by non-Indigenous interests and fundamental to the colonial project of discovery, exploration, and settlement (Carter, 1992; Chapin, Lamb, & Threkeld, 2005; Hemming, 2007; Pratt, 1992; Ryan, 1996; Wolfe, 1999). Natural resource management (NRM) and cultural heritage management (CHM) can be understood as contemporary forms of this ongoing colonialism, and for Ngarrindjeri, experiences with this system have required a program of theorizing, resisting, and transforming these colonizing practices (Hemming & Rigney, 2008, 2010). Critical to this transformative project is a challenge to colonial and colonizing histories of Ngarrindjeri *Ruwe* that frame the relationship between Ngarrindjeri and non-Indigenous people and institutions in South Australia. These colonial histories carry myths of Ngarrindjeri cultural extinction based on Aboriginalist and past-oriented understandings of culture and tradition (Attwood & Arnold, 1992; Berndt, Berndt, & Stanton, 1993; Healy, 2008; Hemming, 2006; Jenkin, 1979). In response, Ngarrindjeri are writing new histories in a variety of settings including heritage reports, management plans, KNY agreements, joint Ngarrindjeri/government NRM programs, and in more conventional historical forums (Bell, 2008; Department of Environment and Heritage, 2009; Hemming, 1994; Ngarindjeri Nation, 2006). Fundamental to these histories is a conception of culture and tradition that is future oriented but respectful of the past, present, and future (Clifford, 2004). This indigenous strategy echoes Arjun Appadurai's call for a shift in understandings of the relationship between development, poverty, and culture. Appadurai (2004) argues that

> we need a sea change in the way we look at culture in order to create a more productive relationship between anthropology and economics, between culture and development, in the battle against poverty. This change requires us to place futurity, rather than pastness, at the heart of our thinking about culture. (p. 84)

The Ngarrindjeri concept of Ruwe/Ruwar encapsulates the connectedness of the lands and waters and all living things and provides Ngarrindjeri with a particular understanding of the links between economy, caring for country, and well-being (Bell, 1998, 2008; Ngarrindjeri Nation, 2006). Like Indigenous peoples in other locations, it privileges the present generation's simultaneous responsibility to the past and the future (Johnson, Louis, & Pramono, 2006). Bringing this ontological understanding into engagements with government and locating it at the center of new relationships built on legal agreements and regional management plans have become the political work of the new Indigenous regional body, the Ngarrindjeri Regional Authority (NRA). As researchers we attempt to support the NRA's leadership in responding to a barrage of complex requests from governments and researchers. We consider, for example, how a new regional body such as the NRA should respond to opportunities to engage with use and occupancy mapping as promoted by the MDBA and MILDRIN. Emerging from these contemporary challenges has been a plan to establish community-based infrastructure to oversee research, program development, and knowledge management (Ngarrindjeri Nation, 2006). This has been identified as critical because of the political, legal, economic, and cultural sensitivities in developing Ngarrindjeri capacity to undertake research projects such as use and occupancy mapping. The Ngarrindjeri prioritization of capacity building can be seen in the Australian Commonwealth Scientific and Research Organisation's (CSIRO) Water-for-a-Healthy-Country Flagship program:

> Ngarrindjeri have their own research aspirations and wish to set priorities to support research which has strategic outcomes to fit into their community development goals, rather than to accommodate research agendas and projects driven by outside academic interests with little reference to the real needs of Ngarrindjeri. (Birckhead et al., 2010, p. 5)

As researchers working for the NRA, key questions emerge based on our experiences with cultural heritage management, native title research, and multidisciplinary research projects (Hemming, 1996, 2002; Hemming et al., 2007; Rigney et al., 2008). If government agencies such as the MDBA promote 'data collection tools' such as use and occupancy mapping, what measures have been put in place to protect the cultural knowledge and intellectual property of the Indigenous communities and individuals involved? When the research is 'completed', who will interpret it? Who writes the overarching management plans? Who gets the final say about their content? What kinds of Indigenous subjectivities will be produced as part of the digital geographical information systems (GIS) databasing projects? Will these research programs be another form of what Deborah Bird Rose (2004) calls 'deep colonization'? Finally, will engagement with another government program lead to increased Ngarrindjeri well-being or become a problematic drain on limited Ngarrindjeri Nation capacity (Hemming & Rigney, 2008)? As Brooke and Kemp (1994) note when writing of the Nunavik Inuit engagement with land use mapping:

> The most important lesson learned from the Nunavik experience is that the indigenous peoples must first and foremost control their own information. It has also become clear over the years that the knowledge base of indigenous peoples is vital, dynamic and evolving. Merely 'collecting' and 'documenting' indigenous environmental knowledge is counterproductive. These knowledge systems have been under serious attack for centuries and the social systems that support them have been seriously undermined . . . It is not a question of recovery and recording indigenous knowledge, it is one of respect and revitalization. (p. 27)

Given the colonial impulse to research, define and control, it is possible that the creation of virtual Indigenous communities through digital databases could lead to the satellization of living Indigenous people in relation to their lands and waters—a dissection of Ngarrindjeri Ruwe/Ruwar and a further act of dispossession (Baudrillard, 1993). The tendency toward containment and simplification that empiricist research linked to digital technology produces often promotes the belief in government contexts, and within the mainstream Australian community, that Indigenous spiritual, social, political, and creative relationships with country are exorbitant, unauthentic, and a threat to the white nation space (Hemming, 2007). Ngarrindjeri have learned hard lessons from their experiences with the power of empiricist research, Aboriginalist myths and patriarchal white sovereignty in the high-profile, cultural heritage issue often labeled the Hindmarsh Island (Kumarangk) Bridge 'saga'. Ngarrindjeri cultural interests were characterized in a Royal Commission, and broadly in the media, as a 'fabrication of secret women's business' to stop development (Bell, 1998; Fergie, 1996; Kartinyeri & Anderson, 2008; Simons, 2003; Stevens, 1995; Trevorrow, 2003). A federal court ruling has since contradicted findings of fabrication, but many Ngarrindjeri leaders remain cautious about the colonizing potential of research (Bell, 2008; Smith, 1999; von Doussa, 2001).

In thinking about the potential value to indigenous people of land use and occupancy mapping we have been drawn to a number of theorists to assist with understanding the affects of engagement with mapping and data-basing practices which 'flow' into indigenous spaces with new technologies that underpin what Michael Hardt and Antonio Negri have characterized as 'Empire' (Appadurai, 1990; Hardt & Negri, 2000, 2004). French theorist Jean Baudrillard identified a shift toward human exorbitance in the context of the network societies or the hyper real (Baudrillard, 1993, 1994). The GIS databases produced in state-desired use and occupancy mapping construct what could be characterized as a hyper colonial social space occupied by virtual Indigenous people potentially acting as a resource for government-controlled NRM. Real Ngarrindjeri, for example, interact with the researchers constructing the maps and databases, but are they subsequently distanced from what Baudrillard defines as a symbolic exchange of meaning inherent in ongoing acts of political negotiation, creative interpretation, or traditional 'consultation' with government officials? Could Indigenous people engaging with use and occupancy mapping be acting as 'double agents of the virtual' to use Baudrillard's phrase, and is this a form of what Rose has described as 'deep colonisation' or hyper colonialism? (Baudrillard in Merrin, 2006, p. 115; Rose, 2004). Manuel Castells' (2007) concept of network society privileges the new media as the social space where power operates. Portions of this digital, social space are fire-walled from everyday interaction and symbolic exchange—they act as new authenticity templates determining what is possible and what is exorbitant (Cohen, 1994). Government-managed GIS databases have the potential to operate in this way. For Hardt and Negri, the indefinability of what they refer to as the 'multitude' (for Baudrillard, 'the masses') remains a hope for resistance to the power of Empire. This indefinability lies at the center of the Ngarrindjeri strategy for survival in a colonizing social spaces (Watson, 2002). For Indigenous people in settler societies the colonial act of mapping, defining, and re-naming has taken on new, hyper colonial forms and requires theorization and new tactics and strategies for resistance or engagement (de Certeau, 1984; Hemming & Rigney, 2010).

CONCLUSION

In the *Handbook of Critical and Indigenous Methodologies* it is argued that Indigenous research must 'meet multiple criteria':

It must be ethical, performative, healing, transformative, decolonizing, and participatory. It must be committed to dialogue, community, self-determination, and cultural autonomy. It must meet peoples perceived needs. It must resist efforts to confine inquiry to a single paradigm or interpretive strategy. It must be unruly, disruptive, critical, and dedicated to the goals of justice and equity. (Denzin, Lincoln, & Smith, 2008, p. 2)

We argue that Indigenous use and occupancy mapping programs should strive to meet the criteria identified by Denzin and colleagues and, in particular, explore the creative capacity of new technologies rather than accepting the empiricist tendencies of GIS databases. We hope that our critical theorization of mapping and new technologies, and their relationship to new formations of colonialism, will assist in an ongoing dialogue about the value of use and occupancy mapping in the development of strategies for positive transformation in First Nations across the Pacific Rim (Barker, 2005; Hemming & Rigney, 2010; Pihama, 2005; Smith, 1999; Stewart-Harawira, 2005).

For First Nations such as the Ngarrindjeri, living in the white heartland of a settler nation-state, the practice of mapping has been traditionally experienced as a Western technology of power and colonialism (Foucault, 1991; Hemming, 2007; Legg, 2005). Land use and occupancy mapping is not new. There has been a long history of attempts by non-Indigenous institutions and individuals to 'map' Ngarrindjeri connections to lands and waters. In the 19th century missionaries 'collected' Ngarrindjeri cultural knowledge and developed social and political maps of Ngarrindjeri 'tribal' lands (Jenkin, 1979; Taplin, 1878). During the 20th and early 21st centuries ethnologists and anthropologists, driven by social Darwinism, salvage ethnography, and more recently cultural heritage and native title legislation, have attempted to research and define Indigenous land use and occupancy (Bell, 1998; Berndt et al., 1993; Hemming, 1996; Hemming, Jones, & Clarke, 1989; Tindale, 1974). As we have argued recently the myth of Ngarrindjeri cultural extinction enabled non-Indigenous experts to act as the new Protectors (following the tradition of appointing Protectors of Aborigines) of the 'relics' and Aboriginal 'sites' of the now extinct or unauthentic Ngarrindjeri people (Hemming & Rigney, 2010).

The danger with digital Indigenous land use and occupancy maps is the potential transfer of authority—the creation of a new kind of Protector. The Aboriginal title or law is being located with another authority—the digital map. The technology, the makers, and holders of technology becomes the keepers of the law and the authorizers of the real. The museumification of Ngarrindjeri Ruwe/Ruwar is at stake once again. In the Hindmarsh Island case, virtual Ngarrindjeri were created by the experts in the museum. In land use and occupancy mapping, virtual Ngarrindjeri, hyper real Ngarrindjeri will be located in the center of government technologies of power, distanced from lived symbolic exchanges of meaning, distanced from the possibility of political action, creative futures, and Ruwe/Ruwar. As Baudrillard (1993) argued, 'Everything which is symbolically exchanged constitutes a mortal danger for the dominant order' (p. 188).

ACKNOWLEDGMENTS

We would like thank the editors of this publication for the opportunity to write this chapter. We acknowledge the support and intellectual contribution of the Ngarrindjeri Regional Authority (NRA) and in particular Ngarrindjeri leaders such as George Trevorrow (deceased), Matthew Rigney (deceased), and Tom Trevorrow. We would also like to thank Shaun Berg, Diane Bell, Chris Wilson, Grant Rigney, Steve Walker (deceased), and Glynn Ricketts for their collegiality and their crucial contributions to developing NRA research and engagement strategies

NOTES

1. Ruwe/Ruwar (land/body/spirit) encapsulates the interconnection of Ngarrindjeri people, their lands, waters, and all living things. This includes the spirits of Ngarrindjeri ancestors.

REFERENCES

Appadurai, A. (1990). Disjuncture and Difference in the Global Cultural Economy. In M. Featherstone (Ed.), *Global culture: Nationalism, globalisation and modernity* (pp.295–310) Thousand Oaks, CA: SAGE Publications.

Appadurai, A. (2004). The capacity to aspire: Cultural and terms of recognition. In V. Rao & M. Walton (Eds.), *Culture and public action* (pp. 59–84). Stanford, CA: Stanford University Press.

Attwood, B., & Arnold, J. (Eds.). (1992). *Power, knowledge and Aborigines*. Melbourne, Australia: La Trobe University Press.

Barker, J. (Ed.). (2005). *Sovereignty matters: Locations of contestation and possibility in Indigenous struggles for self-determination*. Lincoln: University of Nebraska Press.

Baudrillard, J. (1993). *The transparency of evil* (J. Benedict, Trans.). New York: Verso.

Baudrillard, J. (1994). *Simulacra and simulation* (S. F. Glaser, Trans.). Ann Arbor: University of Michigan Press.

Bell, D. (1998). *Ngarrindjeri Wurruwarrin: A world that is, was, and will be*. North Melbourne, Australia: Spinifex.

Bell, D. (Ed.). (2008). *Kungun Ngarrindjeri Miminar Yunnan: Listen to Ngarrindjeri women speaking*. North Melbourne, Australia: Spinifex.

Berndt, R. M., Berndt, C. H., & Stanton, J. E. (1993). *A world that was: The Yaraldi of the Murray River and the Lakes, South Australia*. Melbourne, Australia: Melbourne University/Miegunyah Press.

Birckhead, J., Greiner, D., Hemming, S., Rigney, D., Rigney, M., Trevorrow, G., & Trevorrow, T. (2010). *Economic and cultural values of water to the Ngarrindjeri people of the Lower Lakes, Coorong and Murray Mouth* (CSIRO Water-For-A-Healthy-Country, Flagship Report). Canberra, Australia: CSIRO.

Brooke, L., & Kemp, W. (1994). Towards information self-sufficiency: The Nunavik Inuit gather information on ecology and land use. *Cultural Survival Quarterly, 18*(4). Retrieved April 20, 2010, from http://www.culturalsurvival.org/publications

Carter, P. (1992). *Living in a new country: History, travelling and language*. London: Faber & Faber.

Castells, M. (2007). Communication, power and counter-power in the network society. *International Journal of Communication, 1,* 238–266.

Chapin, M., Lamb, Z., & Threkeld, B. (2005). Mapping indigenous lands. *Annual Review of Anthropology, 34,* 619–638.

Clifford, J. (2004). Looking several ways: anthropology and native heritage in Alaska. *Current Anthropology, 45*(1), 5–30.

Cohen, B. (1994). Technological colonialism and the politics of water. *Cultural Studies, 8*(1), 32–55.

de Certeau, M. (1984). *The practice of everyday life*. Berkeley: University of California Press.

Denzin, N. K., Lincoln, Y. S., & Smith, L. T. (Eds.). (2008). *Handbook of critical and indigenous methodologies*. Newbury Park, CA: Sage.

Department of Environment and Heritage. (2009). *Murray futures: Lower Lakes, Coorong and Murray Mouth*. Adelaide, Australia: Author.

Fergie, D. (1996). Secret envelopes and influential tautologies. *Journal of Australian Studies, 48,* 13–24.

Foucault, M. (1991). Governmentality. In G. Burchell, C. Gordon, & P. Miller (Eds.), *The Foucault effect: Studies in governmentality* (pp. 87–104). London: Harvester Wheatsheaf.

Hardt, M., & Negri, A. (2000). *Empire*. Cambridge, MA: Harvard University Press.

Hardt, M., & Negri, A. (2004). *Multitude*. Cambridge, MA: Harvard University Press.

Healy, C. (2008). *Forgetting Aborigines*. Sydney: University of New South Wales Press.

Hemming, S. (1994). In the tracks of Ngurunderi: The South Australian Museum's Ngurunderi exhibition and cultural tourism. *Australian Aboriginal Studies, 2,* 38–46.

Hemming, S. (1996). Inventing ethnography, *Journal of Australian Studies, 48,* 25–39.

Hemming, S. (2002). Taming the colonial archive: History, native title and colonialism. In M. Paul & G. Gray (Eds.), *Through a smoky mirror: History and native title* (pp. 49–64). Canberra, Australia: Aboriginal Studies Press.

Hemming, S. (2006). The problem with Aboriginal heritage. In G. Worby & L.-I. Rigney (Eds.), *Sharing spaces: Indigenous and non-Indigenous responses to story, country and rights* (pp. 305–328). Perth, Australia: API Network.

Hemming, S. (2007). Managing cultures into the past. In D. W. Rigg (Ed.), *Taking up the challenge: Critical race and whiteness studies in a post colonising nation* (pp. 150–167). Adelaide, Australia: Crawford House.

Hemming, S., Jones, P. G., & Clarke, P.A. (1989). *Ngurunderi: A Ngarrindjeri dreaming*. Adelaide: South Australian Museum.

Hemming, S., & Rigney, D. (2008). Unsettling sustainability: Ngarrindjeri political literacies, strategies of engagement and transformation. *Continuum: Journal of Media and Cultural Studies, 22*(6), 757–775.

Hemming, S., & Rigney, D. (2010). Decentring the new protectors: Transforming Aboriginal heritage in South Australia. *International Journal of Heritage Studies, 16*(1), 90–106.

Hemming, S., Rigney, D., Wallis, L., Trevorrow, T., Rigney, M., & Trevorrow, G. (2007). Caring for Ngarrindjeri country: Collaborative research, community development and social justice. *Indigenous Law Bulletin, 6*(27), 6–8.

Hemming, S., & Trevorrow, T. (2005). Kungun Ngarrindjeri Yunnan: Archaeology, colonialism and reclaiming the future. In C. Smith & H. M. Wobst (Eds.), *Indigenous archaeologies: Decolonizing theory and practice* (pp. 243–261). London: Routledge.

Jenkin, G. (1979). *Conquest of the Ngarrindjeri: The story of the Lower Murray lakes tribes.* Adelaide, Australia: Rigby.

Johnson, J. T., Louis, R. P., & Pramono, A. H. (2006). Facing the future: Encouraging critical cartographic literacies in Indigenous communities, *ACME: An International E-journal for Critical Geographies,* 4(1), 80–98.

Kartinyeri, D., & Anderson, S. (2008). *Doreen Kartinyeri: My Ngarrindjeri calling.* Canberra, Australia: Aboriginal Studies Press.

Legg, S. (2005). Foucault's population geographies: Classifications, biopolitics and governmental spaces. *Population, Space and Place, 11*(3), 137–156. London: Sage.

Merrin, W. (2006). *Baudrillard and media: A critical introduction.* Cambridge, UK: Polity Press.

Morgan, M., Weir, J., & Strelein, L. (2004). *Indigenous rights to water in the Murray Darling Basin* (Research Discussion Paper No. 14, in support of the Indigenous final report to the Living Murray initiative). Canberra, Australia: AIATSIS.

Murray Darling Basin Authority (MDBA). (2009). *Annual report 2008–09.* Canberra, Australia: Author. Retrieved February 5, 2010, from http://www.mdba. gov.au/MDBA-Annual-Report/chapter2-2.html

Ngarrindjeri Nation. (2006). *Ngarrindjeri Nation Yarluwar-Ruwe Plan: Caring for Ngarrindjeri sea country and culture.* Prepared by the Ngarrindjeri Tendi, Ngarrindjeri Heritage Committee, Ngarrindjeri Native Title Management Committee. Camp Coorong, Australia: Ngarrindjeri Land and Progress Association.

Pihama, L. (2005). Asserting Indigenous theories of change. In J. Barker (Ed.), *Sovereignty matters: Locations of contestation and possibility in Indigenous struggles for self-determination* (pp. 191–209). Lincoln: University of Nebraska Press.

Pratt, M. L. (1992). *Imperial eyes: Travel writing and transculturation.* London: Routledge.

Rigney, D., Hemming, S., & Berg, S. (2008). Letters Patent, native title and the Crown in South Australia. In M. Hinton, D. Rigney, & E. Johnston (Eds.), *Indigenous Australians and the law* (2nd ed., pp. 161–178). Sydney: Routledge-Cavendish.

Rose, D. B. (2004). *Reports from a wild country: Ethics for decolonisation.* Sydney: UNSW Press.

Ryan, S. (1996). *The cartographic eye.* Cambridge, UK: Cambridge University Press.

Simons, M. (2003). *The meeting of the waters.* Sydney: Hodder Headline.

Smith, L.T. (1999). *Decolonizing research methodologies.* London: Zed Books.

Stevens, I. (1995). *Report of the Hindmarsh Island Bridge Royal Commission.* Adelaide, Australia: State Print.

Stewart-Harawira, M. (2005). *The new imperial order: Indigenous responses to globalisation.* London: Zed Books.

Strelein, L. (2006). *Compromised jurisprudence: Native title cases since Mabo.* Canberra, Australia: Aboriginal Studies Press.

Taplin, G. (Ed.). (1878). *The folklore, manners, customs, and languages of the South Australian aborigines / gathered from inquiries made by authority of South Australian Government.* Adelaide, Australia: Government Printer.

Tindale, N. B. (1974). *Aboriginal tribes of Australia: Their terrain, environmental controls, distribution, limits, and proper names.* Canberra, Australia: ANU Press.

Tobias, T. (2000). *Chief Kerry's moose: A guidebook to land use and occupancy mapping, research design, and data collection.* Vancouver, BC: Union of BC Indian Chiefs and Ecotrust Canada.

Tobias, T. (2010). *Living proof: The essential data-collection guide for Indigenous use-and-occupancy map surveys*. Vancouver, BC: Union of BC Indian Chiefs and Ecotrust Canada.

Trevorrow, T. (2003). A shocking insult. *Overland, 171,* 62–63.

von Doussa, J. (2001). Chapmans v. Luminis and Ors, Federal Court of Australia, Summary of Judgement, 21 August 2001.

Watson, I. (2002). Aboriginal laws and the sovereignty of terra nullius. *Borderlands e-journal, 1*(2), 1–8. Retrieved March 13, 2004, from http://www.borderlandsjournal.adelaide.edu.au/vol1no2/watson_laws.html

Wolfe, P. (1999). *Settler colonialism and the transformation of anthropology*. London: Cassell.

12 Looking Forward
Diffusing Innovations and Developing Communities With Respect, Dignity, and Justice

Giselle Rampersad, Fay Patel, Prahalad Sooknanan, and Anuradha Mundkur

INTRODUCTION

The rich, vibrant discourse in this book is presented as a point of departure for exploring new and different dimensions to the diffusion of innovations and international development in the 21st century. We share our thoughts on ways in which to be pro-active in the future. In looking forward, we offer suggestions and proposals for enhancing diffusion and international development portfolios and agendas. We invite readers to review our critical perspectives in an attempt to understand our diverse viewpoints and to look through our multifaceted lens. Readers are encouraged to explore, investigate, interrogate, and contest the socio-economic and political landscape on which we want to build our collective dream for a global community founded on the principles of social justice and human rights.

One cannot advocate justice if one has not taken responsibility for providing an environment in which fellow human beings are treated in a just manner. Justice can only be served if one uses the means one has to make a difference to the quality of life of those who are oppressed. We can serve the cause of justice by speaking against injustice, by defending ourselves against those who commit an unjust act upon us, by disapproving an unjust act, by writing about an injustice and exposing it, by thinking about challenging an injustice, or by responding with compassion to those who confront an injustice. Our silence and inability to act locates us with the perpetrators as accomplices of the crime against humanity. As Paulo Freire (1985, p.122) said, 'Washing one's hands of[f] the conflict between the powerful and the powerless means to side with the powerful, not to be neutral'.

MOVING AWAY FROM A DEVELOPMENT PROJECT MINDSET

More significantly, the authors are informed by perspectives grounded in developing and developed community contexts. This is evident from the authors' origins and life journeys (past and present) that stretch across several continents and countries: the United States, Canada, England, New Zealand, Australia, China, India, the Philippines, Indonesia, South Africa, Brazil, and Trinidad and Tobago. It is therefore not surprising that we define ourselves as citizens of the world in an international space where we challenge technological, social, economic, and environmental borders. On account of this awareness, we underscore the need to move beyond the notion of technology transfer from the developed community to developing community contexts. According to McMichael (2004, p. 45) 'not only has the [World] Bank sponsored Western technological transfer, but it has established an institutional presence in Third World countries'. In essence, the editors advocate for a rejection of the notion of the 'development project' and 'the globalization project' (McMichael, 2004, p. xxxix) mindset that has grossly overshadowed the discourse. Within the project paradigm, human development was ignored and underplayed; a missionary zeal overtook the altruistic goal; and the people within the projects were treated as possessions and products to be bartered, exchanged, subjugated, and colonized over and over and over again. The co-editors of the book are all products and victims of 'Third World' projects in the 1970s to 1990s. *Projects* holds a negative connotation because people from 'the projects' are usually impoverished, illiterate, and unable to contribute to mainstream life in a meaningful way. They were in 'the project' that was imposed as part of Western development initiatives, and they remain labeled as being from 'the projects' as a form of branding and as a declaration of their identity. 'The projects' defines who they are, their value, their role, and their potential to make informed decisions about their own lives. The *project* label became a brand name for various politically and economically motivated agendas where whole nations were brought into the fold on the understanding that their emotional and physical well-being and their right to an equitable and sustainable future were the ultimate goal. It is important to note that *projects* continue to be flavored in the Bretton Woods project mold of the early 1940s where the World Bank and the International Monetary Fund were conceived to promote rising living standards on a global scale. Of the 44 nations attending Bretton Woods, 27 were from the Third World (McMichael, 2004, p.45).

INNOVATION AND DEVELOPMENT: AT WHAT PRICE?

'Third World' *projects* such as Bretton Woods remain an important aspect of the current reshuffled loan scheme that resumes the traditional master-servant relationship ensuring that the shackles are never removed from the slaves. The subjects will always return to their masters for more—more food, loans, industrial machinery, technologies—and they will always pay blood money in the form of human life in exchange for diamonds, oil, and water, among other natural resources.

Currently, international development debates continue to echo the colonial paradigms of the past century where decision makers base their summations of the developing community needs on hand-outs, social responsibility budgets, and deficit model biases. Consistent with our advocacy for quality social change, it is imperative that we move this discourse toward investment in the knowledge base, skills, and talents of global citizens in the developed and the developing community context to enable and empower them to sustain future growth and development. To this end, we argue that the renewed focus should be on innovation through human development governed by respect, social justice, and empowerment geared at bringing about sustainable and equitable economic growth with care for the environment. In other words, innovation can be complementary to achieving the goals of health, wellness, food security, energy security, and environmental sustainability. More importantly, innovation should be integrated in a harmonizing manner to secure a sustainable and dignified future for all people. Any form of bonded development is no longer negotiable.

In looking forward, this book brings forth a message of renewed hope to stand firm against all forms of bondedness even when it is cleverly disguised and crafted within *isms* and *izations*: industrialization, technologization, globalization, and imperialism. Throughout the book, forward-looking perspectives are reiterated and reinforced by the authors about reframing and reordering innovation and development discourse to include human development and compassion, harmonizing the manner in which priorities are set and negotiated to achieve the sustainable futures of developing communities. Such harmonization and negotiation must enforce the principles of social responsibility and justice. The process must entrench values of respect and dignity for human life as the fundamental departure point.

The chapters are complex and diverse; however, they focus on the importance of engaging 'other' worldviews that are embedded within unique but valuable cultural knowledge. Further, the authors give voice to histories and identities that have been eroded through the selfish and greedy agendas of hegemonic forces. The perspectives shared in the book highlight the vulnerability of human beings who sacrifice lives, families, lands, and natural resources on an increasing basis in the name of freedom, in exchange for food, and in the hope that their dignities will not be harmed.

Part I of the book brought different perspectives on innovation diffusion and international development. Part II focused on the impact of innovation and development agendas on developing communities, and Part III untangled the web around hunger, poverty, and land dispossessions.

LOOKING FORWARD

Today, a new era for innovation is apparent as the world witnesses a redistribution of wealth and power and a challenge to traditional notions of development and innovation diffusion. Recent events in 2011, such as the Occupy Movement, the Arab Spring and the impact of emerging new mobile technologies are evident of a new era of social change driven by an impassioned global citizenry. Developed and developing communities will continue to challenge injustice with an unparalleled aggression. It is in this regard that innovative solutions are critical in addressing global issues, including environmental sustainability, energy security, food security, poverty, and health and wellness for international development in the 21st century. To this end, suggestions and proposals are presented for further exploration, investigation, and critical review. Most importantly, these suggestions should be assessed against the needs and demands of developing communities and in consultation with them to ascertain whether their contexts will withstand the pressures and force of innovative interventions.

PROPOSALS FOR FUTURE INNOVATION AND INTERNATIONAL DEVELOPMENT INITIATIVES

Finally, it is important to note that this book extends and balances the innovation discourse by adding harmonizing voices of those from both developing and developed communities. In this regard, it is hoped that scholars, consultants, and practitioners of information technology, mass communication, and international development and innovation will be better prepared and informed about their humanitarian roles and responsibilities and about the rights of the developing communities among whom they work. Future innovation and international development initiatives and goals must be aligned to a commitment to the quality of human life and sustainable development among developing communities.

In all chapters, authors have included various proposals, thoughts, and ideas to enhance the quality of life for all by engaging the basic principles of human rights and by establishing a commitment to a sustainable future. The proposals outlined below are possible options for future collaboration and negotiation on innovation diffusion and international development design and implementation in future decades. Of course, it is imperative that the communities who will embrace these initiatives are consulted and their needs and sustainable development priorities remain foremost considerations. Authors offer the following proposals for consideration:

- Proposal 1: Redress the injustices of modernity through the revitalization of a social justice consciousness.
- Proposal 2: Embed the principles of social responsibility, justice, and sustainability within diffusion of innovations and international development initiatives.
- Proposal 3: Adopt a holistic approach to building and sustaining innovative capacity that incorporates institutional, organizational, and individual factors.

- Proposal 4: Advocate for the integration of mainstream and development news as alternative development journalism.
- Proposal 5: Renegotiate gendered spaces to diffuse technology equitably by protecting the rights of all stakeholders.
- Proposal 6: Utilize entertainment-education (E-E) effectively to enhance the quality of life among developing communities.
- Proposal 7: Increase the acceptance levels of SMS-based e-government services by utilizing beliefs and influences as significant factors to enhance the use of services.
- Proposal 8: Seek greater transparency and accountability from all stakeholders in the implementation of e-governance systems.
- Proposal 9: Investigate and apply innovative solutions to foster food security.
- Proposal 10: Address environmental considerations in building energy security effectively.
- Proposal 11: Encourage and facilitate Indigenous community storytelling about Indigenous land use and occupancy while resisting hyper colonial forms.
- Proposal 12: Infuse current and future innovative diffusion and international development design and practice with respect, dignity, and justice.

CONCLUSION

The 21st century will bring new challenges for both developing and developed communities around the world. Practitioners and advocates of diffusion of innovations and international development will have to tread carefully around the minefield of various complex global concerns that include climate change, political upheaval, the containment of infectious diseases, religious and ethnic wars, and economic instability.

It is important to approach the diffusion of innovations and international development initiatives from an informed perspective that recognizes and respects the rights of all human beings to a decent quality of life. The diverse range of cultural knowledge, deeply embedded value and belief systems, and the dignity of all human beings must be respected. Innovative approaches should be explored, especially with the goal of finding ways in which developing and developed communities can continue to live in harmony.

REFERENCES

Freire, P. (1985). *The politics of education, culture, power and liberation.* Westport, CT: Bergin & Gavin.
McMichael, P. (2004). *Development and social change A global perspective* (3rd ed.). Thousand Oaks, CA: Pine Forge Press.

Contributors

Kiran Bains is an Associate Professor in the Department of Food and Nutrition, Punjab Agricultural University, Ludhiana, India. She has 15 years of experience in teaching undergraduate and post-graduate courses in Food and Nutrition. Kiran completed a DFID-sponsored research project with AVRDC (the World Vegetable Center) in Taiwan and another at the National Defence Laboratories in Mysore, India. Her field of expertise is legume research: nutritional analysis, product development, and therapeutic uses. She received the Kellogg's award for Nutritional Excellence twice for research papers presented at the Indian Dietetic Association national conferences. Kiran was a visiting Fellow at the World Vegetable Center, Taiwan in 2003 and at Riddet Centre, Massey University, New Zealand in the years 2007 and 2010.

Tony Susanto is a PhD candidate at the School of Computer Science, Engineering, and Mathematics (CSEM), the Flinders University of South Australia and a recipient of the Australia Leadership Award. Prior to this, he held positions as visiting researcher at the CSEM–South Australia, King Saud University, Saudi Arabia and he was also the Indonesian representative at the IATSS Forum–Japan. Tony's research interests include technology adoption, e-government, and mobile technology and he has presented and published papers on e-government and mobile services.

Robert Goodwin is a Senior Lecturer in the School of Computer Science, Engineering, and Mathematics (CSEM) at the Flinders University of South Australia. He is a research coordinator for Enterprise Information Technology Research Group at CSEM. Robert's research interests relate to the application of information technology in business and education (e-business, e-government, and e-learning) and he lectures in business information systems and computer security. He has published four books on information technology and his articles appear in various journals. Robert has also presented papers at international conferences.

Anil Goorahoo holds a master's degree in Mass Communications (*with Distinction*) from the University of Leicester, United Kingdom. He has been a media practitioner for more than 20 years, having worked in both print and broadcast media. He currently serves as a Media and Communications Advisor to several state and private organizations.

Steve Hemming is a Senior Lecturer in Australian Studies at Flinders University in South Australia. Since the early 1980s he has worked closely with the Ngarrindjeri Nation in the Lower Murray region of South Australia. More recently he has worked with Ngarrindjeri leaders on research projects that address the relationship between natural resource management, Indigenous heritage management, and Indigenous governance.

Anuradha Mundkur has extensive international teaching and practical experience in the fields of gender and development and development communications (including Information and Communication Technology for Development . As the Associate Director of the Gender Consortium, Development Studies, Flinders University, her responsibilities include curriculum design, developing learning and evaluation methodologies, training delivery on gender-sensitive policymaking, implementation and evaluation, research on gender equity issues, and good governance. Anuradha is actively involved in advocating for gender equity through her work with UN Women Australia and as a member of the South Australian Strategic Plan Audit Committee and the South Australian Premier's Council for Women.

Fay Patel is the Associate Director (Curriculum Planning and Student Ratings of Instruction) at Dalhousie University in Halifax, Nova Scotia. Fay has approximately 30 years of teaching, research and management experience in higher education in Canada, Australia, New Zealand, the United States of America , and South Africa . Current research focuses on educational development approaches to online learning, the scholarship of teaching, curriculum development , international development, and the diffusion of information technologies. Fay's co-authored and co-edited publications are *Intercultural Communication: Building a Global Community* (Sage, 2011) and *Working Women: Stories of Strife, Struggle and Survival* (Sage, 2009).

Giselle Rampersad was born in Trinidad and Tobago, West Indies, and holds a PhD in Innovation and Technology Management from the University of Adelaide (Australia), an MSc in Internet Systems and E-Business from Durham University (United Kingdom), and a BSc in Management Studies from the University of the West Indies (Trinidad and Tobago). Giselle is a Senior Lecturer in Innovation and Entrepreneurship and the Coordinator for Business and Technology in the School of Computer

Science Engineering and Mathematics at Flinders University, Australia. Her work has been published in the *Journal of Engineering* and *Technology Management*.

Daryle Rigney is Ngarrindjeri and Associate Professor in Indigenous Studies/Education at the Yunggorendi First Nations Centre at Flinders University in South Australia. Recently he has worked with Ngarrindjeri leaders to develop relationships between Indigenous nations internationally on matters of mutual interest, including cultural and scholarly exchange. He is a co-chair of the United League of Indigenous Nations.

Jan Servaes is the UNESCO Chair in Communication for Sustainable Social Change. He is also the Director of the Centre for Communication and Social Change within the College of Social and Behavioral Sciences at the University of Massachusetts, Amherst.

Prahalad Sooknanan is an Associate Professor of Communications at the University of Trinidad and Tobago. He holds the MA and PhD degrees in Mass Communication from the University of Leicester, UK and Bowling Green State University, USA. Prahalad is a former Visiting Professor at the University of Toledo, Ohio and an Assistant Professor at State University of New York. He is also the local tutor for the MA degree in Mass Communication for the University of Leicester in the West Indies.

Author Index

Subject Index